Information,
Mechanism
and Meaning

Information,
Mechanism
and Meaning

Donald M. MacKay

The M.I.T. Press
Cambridge, Massachusetts, and London, England

Second printing, June 1972

ISBN 0 262 13 055 6 (hardcover)
ISBN 0 262 63 032 X (paperback)

Library of Congress catalog card number: 73-78098

To Claude Curling

Preface

In a day when it is hard enough in most fields of science to keep abreast of new and non-redundant literature, the publication of collected papers, like the estate of holy matrimony, is something not to be undertaken 'unadvisedly, lightly or wantonly'. In the present case it would not have been considered at all but for the kindly initiative of my respected friend Professor Roman Jakobson, whose persistent encouragement alone overcame that distaste which most of us feel for our ten- to twenty-year-old productions and brought this first volume to the point of no return. It is true that these exploratory papers were scattered among an unconscionably awkward selection of publications for anyone wanting to follow them up. On the other hand, as most of them were written for specific occasions, each of which demanded some rehearsal of points covered in earlier essays, the resulting repetitiveness presented a special problem. With occasional exceptions, redundancy could have been eliminated only at the cost of mutilating individual papers. The solution adopted has been to leave almost all repetitive passages intact, offsetting in small print those that can be skipped without loss by readers of the earlier chapters. Where some comment has seemed necessary, by way of foreword or postscript to the original papers, the passages added have been italicized.

With the exception of Chapter 1 (written especially to sketch in the background of the present collection) all the main text has already been published or broadcast over the past twenty years, and I am grateful to the following for permission to reprint:

British Broadcasting Corporation (Chapters 2, 3 and 4)
Josiah Macy Jr. Foundation (Chapter 5 and Appendix)
D. Reidel (Chapter 6)
Butterworths (Chapters 7, 8 and 12)
Harper and Row (Chapter 9)
The RAND Corporation (Chapters 10 and 11)
Verlag Friedr. Vieweg & Son (Chapter 13)
Academic Press (Appendix)
Taylor and Francis (Appendix)

The collection proper falls into two parts, Part I consisting of three introductory broadcast talks and Part II a series of more technical papers. An explanatory survey of the terminology of information theory, prepared for the 1950 London Symposium on Information Theory, has been added as an Appendix. The author's first exploratory paper on 'Quantal Aspects of Scientific Information' (1950) has not been included, partly because its main points are covered in other papers reproduced here but also because I am now less satisfied with it than with any of the rest. Some extracts from this paper appear as part of a postscript to the Appendix, dealing in more detail with the logon-capacity of optical instruments.

It is a pleasure to express my thanks to a number of colleagues whose comments have helped to shape the present collection, to Miss Margaret Steele for tireless secretarial assistance, and to my wife for the considerable labour of compiling the index.

D. M. MacKay
Keele, Staffordshire
December 1968

Contents

Introduction

    Preface   vii

    1. Background   1

Part I. Three Introductory Talks

    2. Measuring Information   9
    3. Meaning and Mechanism   19
    4. What Makes a Question?   31

Part II. Information, Communication and Meaning

    5. In Search of Basic Symbols   41
    6. Operational Aspects of Some Fundamental Concepts of Human Communication   56
    7. The Place of 'Meaning' in the Theory of Information   79
    8. The Informational Analysis of Questions and Commands   94
    9. Communication and Meaning — a Functional Approach   105
    10. Linguistic and Non-Linguistic "Understanding" of Linguistic Tokens   120
    11. Comprehension of Utterances — Some Concluding Notes   128
    12. Generators of Information   132
    13. Indeterminacy, Uncertainty and Information-Content   146

Appendix   The Nomenclature of Information Theory with Postcript on Structural Information-Content and Optical Resolution   156

References   190

Index   193

CHAPTER 1

Background

Towards the end of the Second World War, in the Admiralty's radar establishment, I found myself trying to follow the behaviour of electrical pulses over extremely short intervals of time. Inevitably, one came up against fundamental physical limits to the accuracy of measurement. Typically, these limits seemed to be related in a complementary way, so that one of them could be widened only at the expense of a narrowing of another. An increase in time-resolving power, for example, seemed always to be bought at the expense of a reduction in frequency-resolving power; an improvement in signal-to-noise ratio was often inseparable from a reduction in time-resolving power, and so on. The art of physical measurement seemed to be ultimately a matter of compromise, of choosing between reciprocally related uncertainties.

I was struck by a possible analogy between this situation and the one in atomic physics expressed by Heisenberg's well-known 'Principle of Uncertainty'. This states that the momentum (p) and position (q) of a particle can never be exactly determined at the same instant. The smaller the imprecision (Δp) in p, the larger must be the imprecision (Δq) in q, and vice versa. In fact, the product $\Delta p \times \Delta q$ can never be less than Planck's Constant h, the 'quantum of action'. Action (energy × time) is thus the fundamental physical quantity whose 'atomicity' underlies the compromise-relation expressed in Heisenberg's Principle.

It seemed natural to ask what would happen if one multi-plied together the reciprocally varying quantities in various compromise-relations of the sort I had encountered in experimental measurement. Perhaps these also might reflect the invariance of some fundamental 'quantum'. But a quantum of what? Tentatively, I called it a quantum of *information*. Multiplying together the conjugate pairs of uncertainty-limits mentioned, however, I found that they formed invariant products of not one but two distinct kinds. In one group, the product was a dimensionless number of order 1. In the other, it was a small quantity with the di-mensions of physical entropy. Each of these represented an irreducible limiting factor of experimentation, a 'quantum' more fundamental than either of the two 'uncertainties' of which it was the product.

What then distinguished the two groups? It turned out to be something very simple. The first group of limits, which formed a dimensionless product, were calculable *a priori* (without reference to the measurement actually made), from a specification of the instrument. The second group, which formed products with the dimensions of entropy, could be calculated only *a posteriori*, from a specification of what was *done* with the instrument.

This was in 1945/46. In Autumn 1946 I moved to King's College, London, to teach physics, and a colleague on whom I tried out these notions suggested that there might be a link between my 'quanta of information' and the 'atomic propositions' postulated in Wittgenstein's famous *Tractatus Logico-Philosophicus*. Although in the analysis of ordinary language Wittgenstein himself had now repudiated the atomistic approach of the *Tractatus*,[40] the field of scientific measurement seemed well suited to logical treatment on these lines; for it builds everything ideally upon simple assertions of what Eddington called 'coincidence-relations' and 'occupance-relations' between pointers and scales. At all events, it seemed worth while to explore the possibility that the 'quantization of information' I had stumbled upon in an experimental context was connected with the logical 'atomicity' of the statements that would ideally represent the outcome of the experiment. Was it possible that by analysing the logical requirements for the making of a scientific statement one might find a rational connection between the two kinds of 'quanta'?

As will appear later in this volume, it seemed that one might. A measurement could be thought of as a process in which elementary physical events, each of some prescribed minimal significance, are grouped into conceptually distinguishable categories so as to delineate a certain form (for example, the image on a photographic plate or the wave form on an oscilloscope) with a given degree of precision. In principle, the notion was that each elementary event could justify the addition of one 'atomic fact' to the logical framework representing what took place in ultimate physical terms. For example, any observation pressed to its physical limits could be regarded as an occasion on which the thermodynamic balance of an instrument was disturbed to an extent that could be measured in units of physical entropy. Each of these units, then — suitably defined — could be considered to provide one elementary building-block for an abstract representation of what occurred, the total of such building-blocks being distributed among the various categories or 'degrees of freedom' made available by the instrument, in much the same way as unit events are distributed among the columns of a histogram. Thus the 'informational efficiency' of a given measurement could be estimated by the proportion of those elementary events involved that find themselves represented by atomic facts in a logically adequate statement of the result.

Here then was a possible clue to the meaning of my two kinds of 'quanta'. A scientific representation, viewed in this light, could have its 'size' specified in two complementary ways: (*a*) by enumerating its degrees of freedom, and (*b*) by enumerating its atomic facts. Correspondingly, a representation could be *augmented* in two complementary ways: (*a*) by adding to its degrees of freedom or 'logical dimensionality' (number of logically distinguishable categories); (*b*) by adding to its total of atomic facts or 'weight of evidence' (number of elementary events represented). On inspection, it turned out that the two kinds of quantal limits found in physical measurement represented simply the minimal physical costs of augmenting a representation by *one unit* of the corresponding kind. One could thus speak of a 'unit of information' in either sense as 'that which validates one elementary addition to a logical form representing the result'; but in the first case each unit would add one additional *dimension* (conceptual category), whereas in the second each unit would add one additional *atomic fact*. In order to avoid confusion it seemed appropriate to distinguish the first as 'structural units' and the second as 'metrical units' of information.

It soon became clear that the idea of measuring information was not new. In 1946 Dennis Gabor, then with the B.T.H. Company in Rugby (England), published his classic paper[6] entitled 'Theory of Communication', in which the Fourier-transform theory used in wave-mechanics was applied to the frequency-time $(f \cdot t)$ domain of the communication engineer, with the suggestion that a signal occupying an elementary area of $\Delta f \cdot \Delta t = \frac{1}{2}$ could be regarded as a 'unit of information', which he termed a 'logon'. Much earlier, in 1935, the statistician R. A. Fisher[4] had proposed a measure of the 'Information' in a statistical sample, which in the simplest case amounted to the reciprocal of the variance (see Appendix).

It was far from obvious, on first encountering these disparate concepts, whether they could be fitted in any sensible way into the same framework; but on reflection it became apparent that they were in fact examples of 'structural' and 'metrical' measures, respectively. Gabor's logons, each occupying an area $\Delta f \cdot \Delta t = \frac{1}{2}$ in the $f \cdot t$ plane, represented the logical dimensions of his communication signals. They belonged to the same family as the 'structural units' that occupy an analogous elementary area (the Airy disc) in the focal plane of a microscope, or of a radar aerial. It thus seemed appropriate, with Gabor's blessing, to give the term 'logon-content' a more general definition, as the measure of the logical dimensionality of representations of any form, whether spatial or temporal.

Fisher's measure, which is additive for averaged samples, invited an equally straightforward interpretation as an index of 'weight of evidence'. If we define (arbitrarily but reasonably) a unit or quantum of metrical information (termed a 'metron') as the weight of evidence that gives a probability of $\frac{1}{2}$ to the corresponding proposition, Fisher's 'amount of information' becomes simply proportional to the number of such units supplied by the evidence in question.

Gabor's and Fisher's measures of information were not, however, the only candidates in the field. In 1948, C. E. Shannon published his 'Mathematical Theory of Communication',[31] which proposed for communication signals a measure based on the statistical *improbability* of the signal. Since the logarithm of improbability is additive for independent signals, this obviously had attractive properties. The question was how it related to the 'structural' and 'metrical' measures already in being. Not unnaturally, there was a strong tendency in the late forties to regard all these measures as rivals for a single title, or as suggesting rival concepts of 'information'. A further question was where, if anywhere, the notion of 'meaning' fitted into the scheme of things. Shannon's analysis of the 'amount of information' in a signal, which disclaimed explicitly any concern with its meaning, was widely misinterpreted to imply that the engineers had defined a concept of information *per se* that was totally divorced from that of meaning.

By the time I had plucked up enough courage to publish something on the subject,[12] the outlines of a possible synthesis had begun to emerge, and this was given a trial airing in papers[13] prepared for our first London Symposium on

Information Theory in 1950. Although some aspects of these early explorations may be only of historical interest, a sample is reprinted as an Appendix at the end of the present collection.

Resurrecting and sorting over these twenty-year-old speculations, what strikes one most forcibly is the number of vaguely perceived lines of development, not all of them unpromising, that one has never followed up. The main deflecting factor, it must be confessed, was the lure of a new trail that originated in the conjunction of my interests in information theory and electronic computation. If the concept of information had these dual aspects, the structural and the metrical, what kind of computing mechanism, one wondered, would be best adapted to handle the most general possible transformations of information? In particular, what sort of mechanism must the human brain be, in order to deal as it does with the sort of thing that information is?

Some attempts to wrestle with these problems will appear in a companion volume to the present collection. I mention them now because by the end of 1950 the challenge of the most complex of all computing mechanisms had become my focal interest. A year among neurophysiologists in the United States (1951) completed the transition process; and, for good or ill, most of my remaining half-baked ideas in the field of 'pure' information theory were left to grow cold.

The bulk of the papers in the present volume were written after this change of research emphasis, and they reflect a corresponding preoccupation with information as represented and utilized in the brain and exchanged between human beings, rather than as formalized in logical patterns of elementary propositions. I have not lost hope of a fruitful link between physical and logical atomism in fundamental physics, and it should perhaps be emphasized that the discrediting of logical atomism in the domain of ordinary language has done nothing to diminish its relevance to theoretical cosmology; but the pleasures of matchmaking in this area must be deferred, if not now left to others.

Part I

Three Introductory Talks

CHAPTER 2

Measuring Information

FOREWORD

Future historians of science may find it curious that despite the volume of activity sparked off by Wiener's and Shannon's classic publications in the United States, it was in London that the First International Symposium on Information Theory was held in the summer of 1950. Organized by a small committee chaired by Professor Willis Jackson (now Lord Jackson) of Imperial College, which included a number of enthusiasts for inter-disciplinary collaboration, it became the forerunner of a series of 'London Symposia' which over the next ten years brought together an unusually wide range of scientists, all concerned in some way with systems that depend for their functioning on the transmitting or processing of information.

Such inter-disciplinary meetings, now commonplace, were sufficiently novel in 1950 to excite considerable public interest. The B.B.C. Third Programme talk, the text of which is given below, was an attempt to sketch for a lay audience the ideas and hopes that brought us together on that first occasion. As such I hope that it may be found useful (despite its antique flavour in spots) by readers who feel the need for some gentle introduction to the papers that follow. Those who do not can skip it without loss.

A few months ago there met in London, in the rooms of the Royal Society, a strangely assorted group of people. About a hundred and twenty strong, they included mathematicians, physicists, engineers, linguists, physiologists, geneticists — in fact folk from almost every branch of science

— and they numbered among them representatives from eight different countries.

The subject which attracted us from our various specializations to take part in this unique exchange of ideas was a relatively new one. It is called 'the theory of information', and, as you will have guessed, there are few branches of science about which it has not something more or less useful to say. It is about the new ways of measuring and thinking about information, which we have recently discovered, that I want to speak in this paper.

But, first, why should we want to measure information? There are several reasons. The first is a severely practical one. A scientist is constantly having to choose between different possible ways of tackling a problem. An agriculturalist wants to compare the yields of two kinds of wheat: how shall he plan his experiments so as to get the most out of them for a given expenditure of land or seed? Or, a telegraph engineer wants to design a communication system: which of the many possible varieties will be the most economical for his purpose? What we really want in each case is to discover the method which will give us the maximum *amount of information* for a given outlay of time or space or other resources. There are other reasons for studying the notion of information which will become clearer as we go along; but perhaps the practical one will suffice for the moment.

SELECTIVE INFORMATION-CONTENT

Suppose we begin by asking ourselves what we mean by information. Roughly speaking, we say that we have gained information when we know something now that we didn't know before; when 'what we know' has changed. For example, if we ask a question so simple that it has only two possible answers — yes or no — then we gain information when we receive the answer, yes or no as the case may be. This is the simplest piece of information we can receive; the simplest possible answer to a question with only two possible answers.

Now, if we know there are only two possible answers, we may think of the word 'yes' as an *instruction*, telling us to select one of the two answers. We can carry this idea a step further. We can say that any answer to a question, however complicated, can be reduced to a set of instructions telling us which of the possible answers to select as the right one. We have, in fact, arrived at one of the most important technical senses of the term 'information': that which enables us to make a *selection* from a set of possibilities or to *narrow the range* of possibilities about which we are ignorant. We may use the term 'selective' to distinguish this from other possible functions of information, and it is not difficult to see how this function can be measured. The 'selective information-content' of a message, or of the result of a scientific experiment, for example, has to do with the number of independent choices between two possibilities which it enables us to make — the number of independent yes's or no's to which it is equivalent.

Let me hasten to give you a homely illustration, for this idea is quite simple to see in practice, though difficult to describe in words. Let us suppose that we have two jars of jam on a shelf, numbered one and two, and in one of them the jam has gone bad; we don't know which, but a friend does. We ask him 'Is it number one?' The answer, whether yes or no, provides us with one unit or 'bit' of information, as it is called. It has enabled us to select one out of two possibilities. Imagine now that we were confronted with eight jars of jam, numbered one to eight. If we entered into a kind of 'Twenty Questions' game with our friend, we might begin by asking — Is it one? Is it two? — and so forth until we found the one containing the bad jam. But on the average this is not the quickest way. The most economical method is to divide the jars first into two blocks of four and ask: Is the bad jam in the first block? Then, having discovered in which block it is, we split that into two, and so on. You can easily verify that this method, on the average, leads more quickly to the final answer than any other. So the amount of selective information wrung from our friend in this case is defined as the *minimum* number of choices we've had to make in order to identify the jar of bad jam. And the number of choices is at a minimum if at each stage we arrange to choose between two *equally likely* possibilities. If we do not, then on the average we shall have to ask more questions — without, of course, gaining any more information.

Mathematicians will no doubt recognize at this point that we have really brought in the notion of *probability* in an underhand way. The assumption we are secretly making is that the chances of the bad jam's being in the first block are equal to the chances of its being in the second, provided that we have the same number of jars in each. So before leaving the technicalities (which aren't, perhaps, of great importance in what follows), let us come into the open and admit that we must define 'selective information-content' as the *equivalent* number of independent choices between *equally likely* alternatives. If we didn't make this amendment we might find ourselves saying that the 'amount of information' in a message which we were practically sure of getting was the same as in one which was quite unexpected or improbable.

Descriptive Information-Content

We have so far been talking of situations in which information could be thought of as the answer to a question. It is as if we possessed an enormous filing cabinet containing all possible messages, or results of an experiment, and we regarded our information as instructing us to select the right one. The commonest messages we would arrange, of course, to be the easiest to select — to be picked out in the smallest number of stages.

But I want now to discuss a new kind of situation, in which our problem is not to select but to *build* a picture. Suppose, for example, that we are biologists or physicists looking down a microscope or taking readings on a measuring instrument. Our first problem here is to transform our experience into a symbolic picture or description of what we believe to be the case. Our picture, be it a graph or a drawing, or a scientific statement, depends for its every feature on our actual observations. Each element in the picture therefore formally represents and has its origin in one corresponding elementary feature of the experience pictured. Nothing can legitimately appear in the picture, in other words, unless we have evidence for it by way of experienced observations.

This is an essentially different situation from the earlier one in which we were interested in choosing from a set of ready-made alternatives. Here our picture is not selected, but built up brick by brick, the bricks being provided by our scientific observations. The result is again an addition to what we know to be the case, so we can still say that we are gaining information. But our use of the term here has changed. The apparatus which gives us most *descriptive* information, in this new sense of the term, will be that which yields the largest number of bricks (metaphorically speaking) for our symbolic picture, or which enables us to show the maximum amount of fine structure in it. For example, we may say that a radio signal, whose power we can measure with an accuracy of one percent, gives us more information than one which we can measure only to ten percent, since we can justify the use of more scale-divisions in the first case than in the second to represent our result. Again, we would say that a microscope which can distinguish points one ten-thousandth of a centimetre apart gives more information than one which can only discriminate to one one-thousandth. As a matter of fact, there is an important difference between these two examples. In the first it was the *precision* or *reliability* of our result which we took as a measure of the amount of information it gave us. In the second, it was the number of *distinguishable features* which provided our criterion.

To avoid confusion we have to introduce two more technical terms. When an observation merely increases our reliance on a result, we say it has gained in *metrical* information-content; whereas when we are enabled to add new features to our picture, we say it has gained in *structural* information-content. The two are complementary measures of scientific information, which typically includes both aspects.

But here again the technicalities do not really matter. The point is that we have found a second way of quantifying information, by thinking of it as providing the bricks out of which to build scientific statements. Without information we could not formulate our statements. On the other hand, once a statement has been formulated, we can still regard it as a selection from a range of possible alternatives and so estimate the selective information-content it represents, if we so wish. The three measures of selective, structural and metrical information-content are, in fact, complementary. A very rough analogy of their relationship would be the connection between volume, area and height, as measures of size. We must use whichever is appropriate to our purpose in given circumstances.

Applications of Information Theory

How then do these new ways of thinking quantitatively about information find applications in the various branches of science? Our survey of the theory has been very hasty and rather rough; but if, for the moment, we stick to selective information-content, we can see, I think, the connecting thread. To measure the selective information-content of any body of data, you remember, we ask one standard question. Out of how many equally likely possibilities has this come? If it excludes a large family of other possibilities, so to speak, it 'conveys more selective information' than if it represents one out of only two or three possibilities. And a simple arith-metical rule enables us to calculate the actual amount of selective information in any given case from the number of possible alternatives.

Much of the work on selective information measures has been carried out by telegraph and telephone engineers. The engineer nowadays considers a communication system as a device which can exist in any one of a certain number of possible states. He thinks of a message as something chosen out of a set of possible messages. By thinking in this way, he can calculate precisely how much information his channel could carry in one minute and how much is represented by the message it is actually carrying. In this way it becomes meaningful to talk about the informational efficiency of a telephone channel and to compare, for example, the efficiencies of rival coding systems.

A very similar approach is possible in any situation where information is communicated. Linguists are interested in measuring amounts of information contained in different speech sounds. Physiologists want to know how much information could be carried by a nerve-fibre in a second, how much per second is received by the eye or the ear, and a host of other questions like that. It becomes quite precisely meaningful to ask, for example, whether a particular hypothetical model of the brain could contain as much information as we believe to be held by the real article. In fact, I believe that the ideas of information theory may make a number of real contributions to the study of the brain, which, if nothing else, is a remarkably efficient transformer of information.

In physics, of course, the notion of descriptive information-content is often more useful than that of selective information-content. A physicist may want to know how much theoretically available information is being wasted in a given microscope. He may wish to compare the informational merits of two ways of tackling some problem of measurement. In each case he now has a precise measure of performance, which is sufficiently general to apply to all his possible techniques.

But in physics the concept of selective information-content also becomes interesting, and even exciting, for its own sake. You have probably realized that our method of calculating the number of bits of information, by counting the number of successive sub-divisions required to identify a given choice, amounts to taking the logarithm of the total number of equally likely possibilities. You remember that four jam jars needed two steps and eight jam jars needed three. One out of sixteen jam jars could be selected in four steps, and so on. The number of steps is just the logarithm of the number of possibilities, to the base 2.

Now in thermodynamics this strikes a familiar note. To cut a long story short, our definition of selective information-content turns out to be identical in its mathematical form with the statistical measure of thermodynamic entropy. The units of course are different; but otherwise the only distinction is a difference in sign: where information is given out, entropy increases.

It is possible to make too much of this resemblance; but I think there is no doubt that the famous second law of thermo-dynamics, which states that the entropy of an isolated system tends always to increase, is equivalent in our new language to the assertion that an isolated system can only lose or give out information. And since if a system did not give out information we could never know of it — is the second law really a tautology? I do not know. It is a controversial point. But perhaps now you begin to see why the study of information theory may have an importance quite apart from its immediately practical value.

Of its other more philosophical implications there is not time to say much now. I think a strong case can be made for the suggestion that our concept of time, in at least one of its aspects, is directly linked with the objective notion of the flux of information. If this were so, the concept of time would become meaningless — in fact, could not be defined — for any total system in which the total information remained constant. The presence of an observer, of course, defines an information sink, so that the concept of time must enter directly a system is divided into 'the observed' plus 'the observer'.

The concepts of scientific information are still at a fairly primitive stage of development. There are interesting resemblances, nevertheless, between the types of argument which are applicable in scientific information theory and certain of Eddington's theoretical discussions of the constants of nature. The emphasis in each case is the same — on the nature of the abstract symbolic picture, which we make to represent that which is the case. It remains to be seen how far the two approaches may be inter-related.

I am afraid that in this brief sketch I have given you only some very inadequate glimpses into this new subject and its implications; but we have, I think, seen how it has spun a connecting thread through many disciplines which are otherwise widely separated. At the same time we must beware of the temptation to over-estimate its significance. The theory of information is first and foremost a linguistic tool. It enables us to speak precisely and quantitatively where previously we have had to speak vaguely and qualitatively. It provides objective substitutes for intuitive criteria and subjective prejudices.

But its conclusions are seldom surprising; and it would, I think, be a mistake to place it in the same category as physical theories such as quantum or relativity theory. This is not of course to decry its value, but only to safeguard the theory from mistaken appraisal. If its contributions to science had been only linguistic, their practical results would have already justified the effort which has been expended. But the subject is young, and I think we can confidently look for further developments which, in the end, may even succeed in surprising us.

POSTSCRIPT

Such were the hopes of 1950. It soon became clear that the biggest problem in applying Shannon's selective information measure to human information-processing was to establish meaningful probabilities to be attached to the different possible signals or brain-states concerned. After a flourish of 'applications of information theory' in psychology and biology which underrated the difficulty of this requirement, it has now come to be recognized that information theory has more to offer to the biologist in terms of its qualitative concepts than of its quantitative measures, though these can sometimes be useful in setting upper or lower limits to information-processing performance.

It also became clear that to avoid conceptual confusion it was not sufficient to preface the word 'information' with distinguishing adjectives such as 'selective', 'structural' and 'metrical'. Our chief terminological need was for a way of keeping the notion of information per se *distinct from all measures of 'amount-of-information'. Rather than invent still more neologisms, I took to using 'information-content' (qualified as selective, structural or metrical) to denote the latter, leaving 'information' free to be used in its original everyday sense (see Chapter 6).*

CHAPTER 3

Meaning and Mechanism

FOREWORD

Claude Shannon's measure of selective information-content was framed explicitly to require no reference to the meaning of the information selected in response to a communication signal. The communication process was viewed as a transaction between terminals whose task was confined to the generation and reproduction of symbols. The understanding of these symbols was declared to be outwith the concern of the communication engineers, and the saying went abroad that Information Theory had no place for the concept of meaning.

The second part of this collection (see for example Chapters 5, 6 and 7) contains a number of papers aiming to narrow the gap between semantic and other aspects of the concept of Information as these were gradually hammered out. The text of the talk that follows* outlines a way of thinking about the function of an utterance which these papers use as a conceptual bridge between the mechanistic and semantic levels. By picturing an item of information as a kind of tool that operates upon the recipient's internal 'state of conditional readiness', we can conveniently define its meaning on the one hand, and its information-content (in various senses) on the other. This approach also offers a criterion of meaningfulness and meaninglessness which seems more realistic and less Procrustean than the 'verifiability' or 'falsifiability' criteria canvassed by some linguistic philosophers.

---

* First broadcast in January 1960 on the B.B.C. Third Programme. Reprinted (revised) in *Common Factor*, No. 5, 1968, pp. 57–65.

A human conversation depends on many processes which a scientist would call 'mechanical', in the sense that only physical categories of cause and effect are needed to describe and explain them. Puffs of air, produced by vibration of the speaker's larynx, echo around the cavities of his mouth and result in a characteristic sequence of sound waves. These travel through space and vibrate the sensitive membrane of the listener's ear, giving rise to nerve impulses, and so on. Now, until the chain of explanation reaches the nervous system, nobody minds its mechanistic flavour. True, it has made no reference to the *meaning* of what is being said; but this, we might say, would obviously be premature. Questions of meaning need not arise until we bring in the human links in the chain.

As far as it goes, I think this answer is fair enough; but as a clue to the relation between the meaning of a message and its mechanical embodiment it is far from satisfactory, on two main counts.

In the first place, it seems to imply a rather worrying and muddling sort of discontinuity. The original speaker, we suppose, means something by what he says. His utterance has meaning — at least for him. Yet in the next stages of the chain of explanation (the generation of sound waves and all the rest of it) all signs of his meaning seem to have disappeared. Discussion at this level proceeds in exactly the same terms whether the air is handling the outpourings of a genius or the jabber of a monkey. Yet finally, when the message reaches the ear of a human listener, its 'meaning' seems to pop up again from nowhere, and concerns him far more than the physical properties of the sound wave which the speaker actually produces. There are in fact two awkward discontinuities in this way of telling the story: a jump from meaningful utterance to meaningless air vibrations; and then back again to meaningful utterance. The question that seems to be raised by this way of looking at the process is *how the message recovers its meaning*. Whether or not this is a sensible question remains to be seen.

The second objection to an easy division of human communication into mechanical stages and meaningful stages is a more serious one. The process by which the sound pressure-waves titillate the eardrums is mechanical. So far, so good. But what happens next? Isn't the process by which the nerves convey these titillations to the brain a mechanical one? And what then? Isn't the next, neurophysiological stage, though still puzzling in detail, plainly a mechanical one too? Where are we to draw the line?

The position is complicated by our enormous ignorance of what goes on in the central nervous system. Some people would take advantage of this to suggest that somewhere in the brain the laws of mechanical causation, on which we have been relying, may give place to 'something else' — associated with the action of mind — and this could be the stage at which (as they would say) 'meaning is given' to the buzz of physical brain activity.

For reasons that I won't go into now, I must say I find this suggestion unattractive. To begin with, it seems entirely arbitrary and without scientific foundation, and relies only on our ignorance of brain organization. But my chief objection is that it is an unnecessary way of seeking to safeguard the meaningfulness of human communication — a way that commends itself only if we insist on regarding meaningful and mechanical processes as mutually exclusive, so that to describe something as 'mechanical' implies automatically that it is 'meaningless'. If, as I hope to show, this opposition of 'meaningful' and 'mechanical' is false, the momentum of the whole debate between 'mechanists' and 'anti-mechanists' disappears.

A FUNCTIONAL APPROACH

Suppose we now make a fresh start on the problem of meaning by asking what difference it makes to you when you receive and understand the meaning of a message. For our

purpose it will be sufficient if we confine ourselves to indicative sentences;* suppose, for example, someone tells you
'it's raining'. What happens? You may be immersed in a
book, and may not feel inclined even to grunt an acknow-
ledgement. But this does not mean that your understanding
of the message has had no effect on you. If a sudden call
comes for you to go out of doors, for example, you may now
be ready to reach for umbrella or mac. If someone comes in,
you are likely to ask whether he got wet; and so on. What has
been affected by your understanding of the message is not
necessarily what you do — as some behaviourists have
suggested — but rather what you would be *ready* to do *if*
given (relevant) circumstances arose. It is quite possible that
relevant circumstances may never arise, so that a naively
behaviouristic approach would reveal no sign that you
had understood the message. It is not your behaviour, but
rather your state of *conditional readiness* for behaviour, which
betokens the meaning (to you) of the message you heard.

At this stage you may wonder whether we are not merely
replacing one problem by another — this idea of 'states of
conditional readiness' may sound every bit as vague and
elusive as the notion of meaning itself. The all-important
point, however, is that we can talk about 'states of readiness'
in relation either to human beings or to mechanical systems —
or indeed to human beings as mechanical systems. The notion
offers us a conceptual bridge between the two ways of talking
whose relationship has puzzled us.

Let me try to make it more definite by way of an example.
Think of a railway signal-box controlling a large shunting-
yard. At any given moment, the configuration of levers in the
box defines what the yard is *ready* to do to any waggon that
happens to come along. There may in fact be no waggons
moving; there may be some tracks on which no waggons will

---

* For a discussion of non-indicative meaning in these terms see Chapters
4 to 8 and Chapter 11.

move for years; but this is no obstacle to a definition of the total state of conditional readiness of the yard, as betokened by the total configuration of lever-settings, which determines what would happen *if* any given circumstance arose. A change of a lever that controls a disused siding may cause no visible change in the activity of the yard; but it makes a perfectly definite change in its state of conditional readiness.

Now we do not know at present how the 'signal-box' in our heads controls our own conditional readiness to act and react in all possible circumstances; but it seems reasonable in our present state of knowledge to suppose that there is a brain mechanism that does this. I don't mean of course that the brain is organized on the simple principles of railway signal-ling; there is vastly more subtlety in its blend of spontaneous and controlled activity, which allows us to think of it as determining only the probabilities of different actions in given circumstances, rather than anything as rigid as the motions of railway waggons. What is more, the brain differs from a shunting-yard in being a self-guiding system; and what we are chiefly concerned with is its state of readiness for goal-directed, adaptive activity: activity with a purpose. It is your conditional readiness for this kind of activity that is modified and moulded according to your understanding of the information you receive.

ENERGY VERSUS FORM

But with these cautions in mind, I do suggest that we can think metaphorically of the receipt of a message as causing a change in the 'lever-settings' of the brain, and so in the human receiver's state of readiness, in much the same sense as in the case of our shunting-yard. This will allow us to relate the concepts of meaning and mechanism in a very natural way.

On the one hand, we could say that all that is required to make the brain-levers change is the purely mechanical energy of the message, without reference to its meaning. In one sense this is true. On the other hand, changing the physical energy, say by doubling the loudness, of the message you hear, would not normally make much difference to its effect on your brain-levers; whereas a change in its meaning, even if it left the total energy unaltered, could make all the difference in the world.

The mechanical *energy* of a message must be sufficient to do the mechanical job that eventually resets the brain-levers; but the selective job, of determining which levers shall move, depends on the *form* of the message, and on the state of your brain before you hear it. This is where the meaning of the message comes in. As long as we think only of what actually happens, we may be able to make do with explanations solely in terms of physical energy. It isn't until we consider the range of other states of readiness, that *might have been selected but weren't,* that the notion of meaning comes into its own. A change in meaning implies a different selection from the range of states of readiness. A meaningless message is one that makes no selection from the range. An ambiguous message is one that could make more than one selection.

A Working Definition of Meaning

And so we could go on; but these examples are perhaps sufficient to lead us to a working definition of meaning, in this context. It looks as if the meaning of a message can be defined very simply as its selective function on the range of the recipient's states of conditional readiness for goal-directed activity; so that the meaning of a message to you is its selective function on the range of your states of conditional readiness.

Defined in this way, meaning is clearly a relationship between message and recipient rather than a unique property of the message alone. Thus the conundrum with which we began — the puzzle of the missing meaning — appears to be a spurious one. For the original speaker, the meaning of what he says is the selective function he wants it to perform on the listener's range of states of readiness. This is distinct — and may, as we shall see, be quite different — from the *effective* meaning to the listener, which is of course the selective function actually performed; and both of these may differ from the *conventional* meaning, which is the selective function calculated for a 'standard recipient'. In between the speaking and the hearing — at the stages of mechanical transmission — no comparable selective operations occur, so that questions of meaning do not normally arise; but at any stage we can still define the intended meaning of the message as its intended selective function, and so on. No queer discontinuity occurs along the way.

The jabber of monkeys is thus distinguishable even at the mechanical level from the outpouring of the genius, if we ask the right mechanical question — about its ultimate selective function. Traced far enough along the chain, the effects of the signals emitted by the genius should — or at least could in principle — modify your bodily state of readiness in a manner intended by him; whereas nothing comparable could be said for the sound of monkeys — unless indeed you had some exceptional acquaintance with their vocal habits!

Messages as 'Keys'

Let me now digress a moment to introduce one further feature into our analogy of the signal-box. On the older one-track railway lines, the engine-driver carries a key, which must be inserted and turned in a special signalling lock at the station before his train can be cleared into the next section of the lines. His signal, we may say, is key-operated. Imagine now a complete signal-box, working on the same principle. Insert a key of a given shape into the box, and you make a certain selection from the range of possible configurations of the signal-levers. Insert another, and the selection you make is different.

What I am leading up to is the idea that the brain, considered as a signal-box, is also 'key-operated'. The physical embodiment of a message, which eventually acts on the brain, may be likened to the key that sets up a certain configuration of levers in the signal-box we have been talking about. Its selective function, like that of a key, depends both on its shape and on the arrangement of levers it meets.

It will now be evident that we have sidestepped our second conundrum (about the point in the nervous system at which incoming physical stimuli acquire meaning). From our present point of view, it makes no more sense than to ask about the point inside the key-operated signal-box at which a key 'acquires selective power'. There is, no doubt, a point inside the box at which the 'selective power' of the key is *exercised*; but of course it had this power all along. Similarly, there is, no doubt, a stage in the central nervous process at which the selective function of a message is exercised, and your brain is set up in conditional readiness to match the state of affairs that the message betokens. But we should, I think, rightly decline to regard this as the acquisition of meaning by a hitherto meaningless incoming pattern; for anyone who knew enough of the state and mechanism of your brain (*ex hypothesi*) would have been able in principle to tell that the pattern possessed that meaning for you, even if in fact you never received it. If you know enough about a signal-box, you can determine the 'selective power' that a particular key has for it without ever inserting the key.

Structural versus Functional Criteria

The analogy of a signal-box and key is of course desperately incomplete; for the brain responds to messages in a far more lively way than signal-levers to a key, and its reactions may even include a change in 'code' such that the same key can have different functions on two successive occasions. But the illustration will serve to introduce a topic of recent debate among philosophical linguists and logicians, who are professionally concerned to find an objective basis for talk about meaning. Proponents of one school of thought, whom for short we may call the 'structuralists', concentrate on the structure of what is said, and try to analyse meaning by breaking sentences and words down into their logical components. An extreme form of this approach, advocated at one time by Bertrand Russell,[30] went by the name of 'logical atomism': the idea that the meaning of a complex utterance could be broken down into a conjunction of elementary or 'atomic' sentences, each so simple that it could not be further analysed. Though applicable in some scientific contexts, this notion runs into many difficulties with ordinary language. Advocates of the other school, whom we may term the 'operationalists', look for meaning rather in the pattern of the use that is made of words. This approach is generally associated with the name of Wittgenstein[40] whose later years were spent in vigorous repudiation of the atomistic view of language earlier expounded in his famous *Tractatus Logico-Philosophicus.*

Each party claims an insight into the nature of meaning that the other lacks; and although an outsider here must needs tread delicately, I believe that the mechanistic analogies we have been considering may help us to see not only the justice of these rival contentions, but also the possibility of a unified approach that finds room for both. For a similar argument could be imagined between people on the one hand who wanted to define the 'selective power' of a key by looking at its shape, and those on the other who preferred to watch and see how it was used.

The first, the structuralists, could be quite successful if only all signal-boxes were of a fixed pattern; but if it turned out that some boxes changed their internal arrangement with time, for example, so that the same key had a different selective power at different times, their structural approach would naturally lose prestige. The second, the operationalists, would be in their element if keys behaved in a way that could not be predicted from their structure; but if in fact most keys of a certain shape were found consistently to make a selection predictable from that shape, their operational method would seem very roundabout and inefficient and lacking in insight.

As a parable of the situation in semantics this is a little unfair, but it will serve our present purpose. In each case, I think, trouble arises through taking an experimental *criterion* as an objective *definition*. Both the structure of a key and the pattern of its use are necessary experimental pointers to its 'selective power'; but neither is suitable as an overall definition of the notion. Similarly, both the structure of a message and its pattern of use would seem to be necessary experimental pointers to its 'meaning'; but we only breed confusion if we try to turn either of them into a definition of what they betoken.

Does our mechanistic analysis offer any clues, then, to a synthesis between these rival lines of thought? Let us recapitulate briefly. We have been thinking of human communication in terms of the mechanical pattern of cause-and-effect that we have assumed to embody it from start to finish. We have considered the human recipient's brain as a physical system, with at any time a certain (statistical) 'state of conditional readiness', roughly analogous to what we called the 'state of conditional readiness' of a railway shunting-yard. The object of communication is to select some particular conditional readiness in the recipient from the range of states that are possible. The intended meaning of the communication is then definable as the selective function that it is intended to exercise on the range of possible states. Its effective meaning is the selective function that it actually performs.

SEMANTIC UNITS AND CRITERIA OF TRUTHFULNESS

Now the big difference between the brain and a signal-box, of course, comes in here; for, as we noted, the effect of an input to the brain is liable to depend in a complicated way on what has gone before it; and it is only in special cases, usually after long training, that one could rely on getting exactly the same effect from the same input at different times. The moral — and it is an important one — is that what we may call the 'semantic units' of communication — corresponding to the keys we have been talking about — are often made up of a whole group of words or even of sentences acting together, rather than single words acting in isolation. The selective job is done in easy stages, as it were, and the final sharpening-up of the state of readiness may sometimes have to wait a long time for some of the words necessary to complete it. (This is particularly true, of course, in poetic and religious forms of speech — but that's another story.)

It might be argued on these lines that the concept of semantic unit must be extended to include the whole linguistic experience of the listener; but this in most cases would be unrealistic. Our point is simply that in many quite ordinary cases the unit of communication can and does extend far beyond the boundaries of a grammatically complete and apparently unambiguous statement, so that it becomes unrealistic to attach labels such as 'true' or 'false' to the particular statement in isolation. For truthful communication, what matters is whether the present message, coupled with what has gone before it, is calculated to select a state of readiness to match the actual state of affairs. If it is not, then the communication is untruthful, regardless of whether we would be inclined to accept its component sentences as true if we took them in isolation. It is easy to see from a mechanistic angle how even a physical change in tone of voice might alter the state of readiness selected from an appropriate one to an inappropriate one. I can deceive you by telling you the truth, if I do so in such a way that I know you will not believe me. More insidiously, of course, I can do so by simply selecting 'true information' which I know will give you a false impression in the absence of other data. In short, by insisting that criteria of truthfulness should be applied to semantic units rather than to statements, we demand an even higher standard of honesty in human discourse than is achieved by simple propositional logic.

In the end, then, we find ourselves agreeing with both the 'structuralists' and the 'operationalists'. Meaning is indeed inseparable from use, for it is a relation between message and recipient which may differ from one recipient to another. Thus far our sympathies must be with the operationalists. On the other hand, provided that we consider semantic units instead of words, we can agree with the 'structuralists' in believing that the structure is a major determinant of selective function. Different though they are in detailed contents, our brains embody basic principles of organization that have to be reckoned with — and in that sense reflected — in any linguistic system. Indeed I would go so far as to hope that when — if ever — the outlines of the 'shunting-yard' of our brains become a little clearer, one of the tools that will help us further to unravel its structure may well be the analysis of human language.

POSTSCRIPT

A standard source of the line of thought we have called 'operational-ist' is Wittgenstein's Philosophical Investigations.[40] *A more 'structuralist' approach is taken by Ullman in* The Principles of Semantics.[38] *Contemporary trends may be followed in:* The Structure of Language, *edited by J. A. Fodor and J. J. Katz.*[5]

A recent general review entitled 'Opinions about Language' is given in: What is Language? — A New Approach to Linguistic Description *by R. M. W. Dixon.*[3]

CHAPTER 4

What Makes a Question?

In our search for a conceptual bridge between mechanism and meaning, we have so far considered only indicative sentences. The third of these introductory talks* tackles the problem of defining the meaning of interrogative utterances in a mechanistic context. The notion of 'conditional readiness' is here illustrated in terms of a switchboard (of a rather indeterministic sort) instead of a signal-box; but the approach is essentially the same as in Chapter 3.

Asking questions, like walking, is something we learn to do from infancy — as every parent knows all too well. It comes so naturally, in fact, that to ask how we do it may seem more than a little queer. And yet, when you think about it, there is something rather remarkable about this ability of ours to coax or wring information out of one another just by uttering a few words of our own; and when you come to study communication between human beings from a scientific point of view, as the new science of 'information theory' tries to do, it is not at all obvious what distinguishes a question from all the other noises a man can make, or how to describe the process by which questions produce the effects they do. This is the problem I want to discuss — the problem of describing scientifically how questions work.

* Broadcast on B.B.C. Third Programme and first published in *The Listener*, May 5th, 1960.

Form and Intonation

I suppose our first guess might be that the peculiar nature of a question lay in its grammatical construction. It is a fact that nearly all our questions are expressed in a special form: for example, we turn the indicative: 'You are going home' into the interrogative: 'Are you going home?' The order of subject and verb is reversed. In many cases this kind of clue is indeed sufficient to mark the utterance as a question. But what if someone simply says, 'Going home?' I do not think you would doubt that he was asking you a question; yet the very same words, with a different intonation, could also be the *answer* to a question: 'Where are you off to?' — 'Going home'. Evidently grammatical form, though a useful clue in most cases, is not the essential distinguishing feature of a question. In idiomatic speech particularly, the intonation may sometimes be the thing that matters most. We can think of the questioning intonation, in fact, as a kind of vocal equivalent of the question-mark. Incidentally, have you ever thought how much richer and less ambiguous our printed language would be if only we had an easy way of representing intonation — say by making letters larger and smaller, or tilting the lines up or down? We lose much of the information-content of speech by printing it.

Our examples so far have all had some peculiarity, either of grammatical form or of intonation, that marked the utterance as a question. But now what about the man who says: 'I take it that you are going home'. Is he asking a question? Here the grammatical form is plainly indicative and not interrogative; and his utterance of it can be as flat as you like. A computing machine programmed only to distinguish questions by their form would be foxed here. Yet it would make perfectly good sense for you to treat it as a question and reply: 'Yes, I'm just on my way', or 'No, I'll be around for a few minutes yet': just as if he had asked the direct question, 'Are you going home?' In fact, this response of yours not only makes sense but it is what would normally be expected of you. I mean, if he were to say: 'I take it that you're going home', and you were to reply 'All right; so you take it that I'm going home' — he would not think you were playing the game at all.

AN INCOMPLETE PICTURE

What has he done to you (as distinct from the computer), by making this purely indicative statement, that gives him any right to expect an informative reply? What does his statement have in common with the interrogative form of question to which he is really wanting an answer? Here I think we come to the root of our problem. What he has done, by making his indicative statement, is to expose to you a certain incompleteness in his picture of the world — an inadequacy in what we might call his 'state of readiness' to interact purposefully with the world around him and specifically with yourself. He is only assuming that you are going home. If he knew that you were going to be about for some time, he would perhaps be ready to call on you if he needed help, ready to leave the lights on in the hall if he were going out, and so forth. If, on the other hand, he knew you were going home, he would be ready to act quite differently in these various circumstances. It is rather as if he had a whole series of switches in his brain, needing to be set one way if you are going home, and the other way if you are not. His state of readiness is incomplete until these have been set.

It is perhaps hardly necessary to say that the human brain is not as simple as a switchboard, even of the complicated automatic sort you would find in an electronic computer. What goes on in it is far less cut-and-dried, far more spontaneous and undisciplined, than an engineer could tolerate in a switchboard. In place of the virtual certainty with which a switch operates, the brain cells offer only a certain probability that they will send signals one way rather than another. So if we were going to be accurate we would have to describe a man's state of readiness in terms of a large number of what the theorist calls conditional probabilities — the probabilities that if he wanted to do such and such, in given circumstances, he would set about it thus and so.

With this qualification, I think the idea of switch-settings in the brain is not a bad way of picturing the mechanisms that embody our 'states of readiness'. It provides us with a useful metaphorical way of looking at a question, as an opportunity presented to someone else to set some of the switches for the questioner. It is as if the questioner uncovered and held out the incomplete part of his switchboard to the listener, in the hope of having the switches set for him.

AN ESSENTIAL PRESUPPOSITION

This brings out an essential presuppostion behind the whole business: namely, that the exposure of an incomplete or incorrectly set switchboard is normally a stimulus to action on the part of the receiver: that human beings are motivated to set one another's switches; or, in more psychological terms, to adjust one another's states of readiness, just as they are motivated to help one another in other ways. Call it, if you like, filling up one another's world map. I do not want now to discuss the reasons for this. We may be moved by the purest wish to be helpful, or by its tiresome twin, the longing to put other people right. Part of what makes us people is our readiness to interact with one another in this way. No doubt one could argue that if we did not have a mechanism of this sort built into us the race would hardly have survived. But that is by the way. The point to note is that we cannot define an utterance to be a question simply on the ground that it has moved someone to adjust the speaker's state of readiness, because people are liable to do this spontaneously, and may sometimes get no thanks for their pains.

Where then does this take us? What we have established is that a question is a combination of an indication and an invitation, which we have likened to the uncovering of a switchboard, whereby the questioner seeks to have some of his switches set for him by the receiver. Instead of passively regarding it, as he might the back of a bus, the receiver reacts to the uncovered switchboard as a target for his activity. He sets to work to try to alter or to complete the switch-settings that have been displayed to him. He may judge that he has been invited to do this either from the manner of the uncovering or from the circumstances.

The usefulness of this rather long-winded way of expressing common-sense facts is that it has brought us clean away from any necessary reference to grammar or even to language. There are all sorts of wordless methods of displaying an inadequacy, and plenty of wordless conventions to indicate readiness to have it remedied, from the extravagances of comedians in the old days of the silent film, to the discreetly inquiring lift of an eyebrow. As we have already seen, the mere fact that the speaker has chosen to display the inadequacy to the receiver may be a sufficient indication that help is being asked. At the mechanical level, I dare say the process has some analogy with the way a mother bird's reactions are stimulated by a gaping beak in the nest — the big difference being that our responses have to be learned.

LOOKING FOR A DEFINITION

Suppose we try in this context to define the meaning of a question. I have suggested in the previous talk that the meaning of an indicative sentence to a receiver might be defined in terms of the state of readiness it sets up; or, more precisely, as its selective function on the range of the receiver's possible states of readiness for goal-directed activity. For short, I suggest we call this its organizing function. Thus the sentence 'It is raining' selects in you a whole complex state of readiness to take umbrella or mackintosh if you go out, to shut a window if you see it wide open, and so forth.

We can picture this effect as the setting of a whole series of the brain-switches we have been talking about, which govern what you are likely to do in all relevant circumstances. You may notice that we are not defining the meaning as the change produced in you, but as a relation between the utterance and yourself, which we have called its organizing function. Meaning is always meaning *to someone*.

The main purpose of a question is to bring about, by remote control as it were, a change in the questioner's own state of readiness. He is trying to get some of his switches set for him. The primary meaning of a question, then, which we might call its interrogative meaning, can be defined as its selective function on the range of the questioner's states of readiness for purposeful activity, or, for short, its organizing function for the questioner. Its job is to identify the switches that need setting. The meaning of the answer will be a selective function on the same range but a more detailed one. Its job is to set the switches.

On the other hand, as we have seen, a question also plays an indicative role, by simply showing the receiver the state of the questioner's switchboard. We might therefore define the indicative meaning of a question as its organizing function on the receiver's readiness for the state of the questioner's switchboard. One further distinction we must obviously make is between the organizing function actually exercised in each case — the effective meaning — and that which was intended by the questioner.

CRITERIA OF MEANINGLESSNESS

All this leads up to a topic of fierce debate among philosophers nowadays: When is a question meaningless? Some people would argue that a question is meaningless unless one has some physical way of verifying the answer to it. For them, the whole of metaphysics and theology are worthless on this score, and questions of the kind 'Does God exist?'

can simply be ignored. At the other extreme are those who would admit any question to be meaningful if people in fact ask it.

Our own first answer has to be that a question is meaningless when it has no organizing function. But we must go on to distinguish again between interrogative and indicative meaning. Interrogatively, a question is meaningless when it *calls for* no organizing operation. Indicatively, it is meaningless when it *has* none. We can also distinguish in obvious ways between meaninglessness to the receiver and to the questioner. As a basic criterion of meaninglessness, this 'absence of organizing function' is I think a good deal more realistic than either of the extremes I have mentioned. On the one hand, it rules out questions whose components have either no selective function or mutually incompatible selective functions, whether or not people have been accustomed to asking them. On the other hand, it gives no excuse to stifle any metaphysical or theological questions that have a bearing, however remote, on experience or action.

Thus to ask: 'Where does the flame go when the gas is turned off?' is interrogatively meaningless as it stands, because if we assume that 'flame' means 'gas being burned', the two halves of the question contradict one another: they call for mutually incompatible selective functions. When there is no gas, there is no flame to go anywhere. But it is not indicatively meaningless, because its utterance does convey a picture of the questioner's muddled switchboard.

On the other hand, questions of the kind: 'Does God exist?' may well seem indicatively meaningless to a non-religious person who has no means of knowing what kind of inadequacy, if any, they betoken. Yet, inasmuch as the questioner's whole apparatus of motives and conduct — not to mention his experience — can depend radically on the answer, such questions can scarcely be termed interrogatively meaningless. Their answers, whether true or false, are going to affect switchboard-settings for the whole of his life.

There is, however, one kind of nonsense-question that might seem to slip through our net. I mean the sort of question that is asked and answered only in terms of an artificial language with no relation to reality — a kind of game without meaning. Here one might argue that the questions ought still to be called meaningful, because they do have a bearing on activity of a kind — namely the activity of talking the artificial language. To avoid a wrangle, I would be prepared to concede this, but on condition that where the only readinesses affected by talking a language are readinesses to talk more of the same language, it should be termed only artificially meaningful. I think it was a horror of this kind of artificial, empty meaning that led some people to try to define sentences as meaningless unless they admitted of physical verification. But I hope I have shown that such Procrustean measures are not necessary in order to have a working idea of what makes a meaningful question.

Part II

Information, Communication and Meaning

CHAPTER 5

*In Search of Basic Symbols**

FOREWORD

"*Information is as information does*" — *such is the watchword of the operational theory of information. Where it selects or constructs tangible representations, information is easy to measure, at least in principle. But what happens when information is absorbed by a human recipient? Can we think of analogous selective or constructive processes going on inside his brain? If so, what might we suppose to be the elements — the basic symbolic alphabet, so to speak — upon which such operations could take place?*

These were the main questions intended to be raised by an informal talk under the above title, portions of which are here reproduced more or less verbatim from the proceedings of the 1951 Josiah Macy Jr. Foundation conference on Cybernetics. These enjoyable occasions were noted for their rumbustiousness, and as it turned out a good deal of time had to be devoted to explaining and arguing the need for different but complementary measures of information-content; so the semantic aspects had to be crowded into an inadequate few minutes at the end. Although the extracts that follow give only a sketchy indication of what was in mind, they may help to show how a formalism originally developed to represent the information derived from a scientific measurement led to exploratory questions in a more general context.

* *Proc. 8th Conf. on Cybernetics* (H. von Foerster, ed.) Josiah Macy Jr. Foundation, New York, 1951, 181–221.

General information theory is concerned with the problem of measuring changes in knowledge. Its key is the fact that we can *represent* what we know by means of pictures, logical statements, symbolic models, or what you will. When we receive information, it causes a change in the symbolic picture, or *representation*, that we could use to depict what we know.

We shall want to keep in mind this notion of a representation, which is a crucial one. Indeed, the subject matter of general information theory could be said to be the making of representations — the different ways in which representations can be produced, and the numerics both of the production processes and of the representations themselves.

By throwing our spotlight on this representational activity, we find ourselves able to formulate definitions of the central notions of information theory which are operational, with more resultant advantages than just current respectability. In any question or debate about "amount of information", we have simply to ask, "What representational activity are we talking about, and what numerical parameter is in question?" and we eliminate most of the ground for altercations, or we ought to do so if we are careful enough!

Our first concern must be to make enough distinctions and provide ourselves with an adequate enough vocabulary to avoid major trouble.*

Representations commonly originate in two distinct ways. The difference between these is the essence of one of the most important distinctions in information theory — between the *theory of communication* on the one hand and what for want of a better term we may call the *theory of scientific information* on the other. Both a communication-process and a scientific observation-process result in the appearance of a representation in the "representation-space" of the receiver or observer. But what distinguishes communication, I suggest, is the fact that the representation produced is (or purports to be) a *replica* of a representation already present to (with, in-the-mind-of) the sender. Communication is the activity of *replicating representations*.

* An explanatory survey of some key terms of information theory (as of 1950) is reprinted as an Appendix.

This is to be contrasted with the typical activity of physical scientific observation of which the goal is the making of a *new* represention, representing some additional knowledge of that-which-is-physically-the-case concerning some unique space–time tract not heretofore represented anywhere.

We might put it crudely as the distinction between the replication and the formulation of knowledge. The problems raised in the two cases are in some respects quite different and give rise (as we saw in Chapter 2) to different "measures of information".

Now it is evident that in any situation in which what is observed is thought of as specifying one out of an ensemble of preconceived possibilities, the amount of selective information so specified can in principle be computed (see Appendix). Shannon's concept has, therefore, a much wider domain of usefulness than that of communication theory. The point is that it is always a relevant parameter of a communication-process, because successful communication depends on symbols having significance for the receiver, and hence on their being already in some sense prefabricated for him. The practical difficulty, of course, is to estimate the proportions of the appropriate ensemble, when these are determined by subjectively and even unconsciously assessed probabilities.

SCIENTIFIC INFORMATION

But now let us turn to this other problem which faces the physicist: namely, making a represention of that-which-is-physically-the-case concerning some tract of space–time. This I have discussed at length elsewhere (see Chapter 1 and Appendix), and I want here only to outline the kind of formalism which is useful to represent the processes concerned.

In this case, we are not usually in a position to select from a filing-cabinet of preformed representations; we have to produce our representations *ab initio*. Our scientific representation is in general compounded of elements portraying certain relations, say between the magnitude of a voltage and a particular point on a time axis, or between the intensity of transmitted light and a particular coordinate-intersection in the field of view of a microscope. We say "the voltage was 10 volts at time t_1, 10.5 at t_2" and so forth.

Our ability to name operationally a certain number of distinct coordinate values, such as t_1 and t_2, enables us to prepare in advance the same number of distinguishable, independent "blank statements" of the form: "The magnitude had the value such-and-such at coordinate-point q_n" or, rather, "The magnitude had the average value such-and-such over the coordinate-interval Δq around q_n", and so on. The blanks in these statements or "propositional functions" we then fill in as a result of our observations.

We are thus clearly faced with a two-fold problem: First, we must be able to *define* distinguishably in operational terms the blank statements which we want to prepare. In other words, something in the design of the experimental apparatus or procedure must enable us to identify and distinguish between observations if we want to call these observations "independent" or even "distinct".

Second, we must collect *evidence* for our statements by observation of events. We "plug in" observed data, so to speak, into the blank spaces which we have for them in our previously prepared propositional structure. If we boil a typical statement down to the over-simple form "value X relates to interval Y", then our two problems are the *operational definition of Y* and the *collection of evidence for X*.

Now a set of independent propositions can be represented or symbolized by a set of perpendicular axes in a multi-dimensional hyperspace. So we can represent the additive process by which information accumulates with the help of a convenient geometrical vector-model, in which for each new independent proposition we add one dimension to our hyperspace — our "information-space". We then can take *distance* in each of those dimensions to represent some function of the amount of metrical information (see Chapter 1 and Appendix) associated with the corresponding proposition.

If each structural proposition is represented by a vector whose length is the square root of its metrical information-content, then the total information-content, structural and metrical, is represented by the vector sum of the individual components.

For example, if we had just two propositions, we could define their total information-content by drawing a single vector whose two perpendicular components are the square roots of the amount of metrical information in each. In the particular case of voltage measurement, the two propositions concern two successive independent readings, and these vector-components are actually proportional to the signal–noise voltage ratio. In that case, of course, the square of the length of the resultant is the sum of the squares of the lengths of its individual components, and is proportional to the total energy, so we get a representation in which additivity is preserved.*

COMMUNICATION

If now we had to communicate a representation like this to somebody else, we could think of our activity as instructing him to select, out of a certain number of possible positions for the information vector, one representing the result that we have obtained. The tip of the vector can be represented as occupying one of a number of cells into which the space is divided or quantized. In that case (on the assumption that each position is equally probable for the sake of argument), we can take the logarithm (base 2) of the number of possible positions out of which our result has selected one, as a measure, first, of the number of binary decisions to which this selection is equivalent and, hence, as a measure of the amount of information in Shannon's sense, which you remember we distinguished by calling it the selective information-content.

---

* This assumes a constant "noise" level per degree of freedom. The case where the noise level is different for different degrees of freedom requires an extension to the formalism which was never undertaken.

In communication between human beings, and possibly between animals, the problem is ultimately the production in one reasoning-mechanism of a representation — a pattern — already present in another reasoning-mechanism. In the human case the communication engineer is interested especially in the most economical way in which we could transmit the selective operation that evokes the appropriate pattern; and, since we can do this by coding, we are always prepared in principle to take the logarithm of the total number of equiprobable possibilities as our measure of the "amount of information" given, irrespective of the properties of the pattern signified.

In the other process, the process of scientific observation in which we are confronted by a situation about which we are initially wordless, our experimental method — our mode of approaching the situation — has to provide us with both (*a*) the conceptual possibility of formulating — giving distinguishable significance to — a certain number of propositions, and (*b*), as a result of observing events, the ability to adduce evidence for these propositions.

Meaning

Now, what about the concept of meaning? Suppose we forget for the moment about signals, which are very often symbols for something else, and just take the case of two propositions. In ordinary mathematical logic, one could say that, if you assert two independent propositions A and B, you have said something which is equivalent to the logical combination of these two, which could be symbolized, therefore, as a point in a diagram with four possible positions (Fig. 1). In position 1, you have said both. In position 2, you say "A" but not "B"; and so on. So the statement you make could be defined by a vector, the vector linking these points to the origin, which has four possible quantal positions.

Now it is common experience that we do not fully define

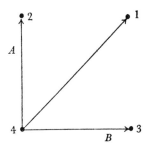

Fig. 1.   A vectorial representation of the four possible conjunctions of two
independent all-or-nothing propositions *A* and *B*

many of our concepts in terms of a set of discrete, yes-or-no propositions. The concept of a chair is not definable simply by enumerating a certain number of characteristics, because we all know that if a chair doesn't have a leg, we may still judge that it is a chair which has lost its leg, or something like that. I believe that according to some linguistic philosophers the most you can do is to enumerate a set of possible characteristics of chairs, of which any adequate sub-selection constitutes a chair where found. What we need, it seems, is some way of symbolizing the *partial participation* of one or more characteristics in a definition. The black-and-white of atomic, yes-or-no components is too coarse for our everyday terms.

Partial Participation

Can we then sharpen-up this notion of "partial participation"? What could we mean by saying that a certain term means "a little of *A* and a lot of *B*", instead of accepting the four-way choice offered to us by conventional logic in Fig. 1 ? Suppose we try to say that the meaning of a term represents, not a discrete selection from a set of "yes-or-no" characteristics, but a selection of each *in a certain proportion*; what reasonable meaning could we give to that?

What we could mean, I suggest, is that our definitions are to some extent ostensive — that their meaning is acquired from experience. In the past over which a given term has acquired certain associations to which we point implicitly or explicitly when we use it, we may have found that *A* was associated only 10 times, say, and *B* 100 times, so that the term *means* in this sense "a little of *A* and a lot of *B*". If you like to picture the elementary characteristics as spread out along a scale, the meaning of a term becomes a kind of spectrum — a spectral distribution — over the scale, the relative frequencies of occurrence of the different elements being symbolized by the height or intensity of the spectrum over the corresponding points on the scale.

I wonder if I am making that clear? The idea is that if you make a list of features of chairs: having legs, having backs, and what not; then some chairs are backless, some chairs have no legs, and so on. So if we accept these (for the sake of argument) as simple "yes-or-no" characters, then over a long experience of the word "chair" we should build up a concept of "chairfulness", which could be defined by the proportions of different characters in the ensemble of all chairs experienced.

The interesting thing is that this possibility would correspond in our vector-model (Fig. 1) to attributing significance to *all* orientations of the vector. Instead of having merely the possibility that the vector is vertical, horizontal, or inclined at 45 degrees, we now have the possibility of conceptually infinitesimal gradations of orientation. Quite precisely, what corresponds to the *meaning* of a given term which is definable in terms of this space of basic vectors (elementary component characters) is the *orientation* of its representative vector — the direction which defines the relative weights with which those elementary components enter into our experience-based understanding of the term.

It is possible, of course, to use different metrics here. We could arrange that as the probability of inclusion goes from 0 to 1, so length only goes from 0 to 1, as in quantum theory. But if we are dealing in terms of metrical information we make no restriction, and the length could go to infinity (which would be equivalent to an infinite weight of evidence).

The choice of metric for our purpose is not particularly important. The point is that with a given metric we can have a precise representation of the *meaning of a statement for a given individual*, remembering that each individual receiver will have his basic vectors defined by his own internal apparatus. Different *shades* of meaning are represented by different orientations within the same subspace. The *relevance* of evidence to a dependent statement is represented quite precisely by the square of the cosine of the *angle* between the two corresponding directions in information-space, in that the weight of evidence afforded to a dependent statement by a given body of information is found by squaring the projection of the information-vector on the ray which defines the statement.

THE RECEIVER'S INTERNAL REPRESENTATION OF INFORMATION

Perhaps I can best introduce the question of the receiver's internal representation of information by presenting to you the bare bones of a possible general-purpose reasoning mechanism,[11,14] which we want to be capable not only of dealing in black-and-white logic, but also capable of receiving and representing and reacting appropriately to the kind of information we have been talking about — information in the general sense. Essentially, this is a probabilistic mechanism, in which "trains of thought" (metaphorically speaking) correspond to transformations of information-vectors which may be continuous or discrete.

The main things we are going to need are, first, some means of symbolizing probability, of representing probability appropriately in our mechanism; and, second, some way of representing the basic vectors or dimensions of information-space: the elementary components, the basic symbols, out of which such a mechanism could build its representation of a universe of discourse.

It will be easiest I think to leave the probabilistic question to the last, and consider first how the computing machinery of an organism reacting with its environment might derive its internal "descriptive alphabet" of elementary symbols. As I see it, we have a basic choice between (*a*) the use of the *incoming stimuli* or filtrates thereof, and (*b*) the use of the elementary *acts of internal response* to received stimuli, as symbolic components for the internal representation of what is "perceived". So this is our first question: Does one's internal representational mechanism describe an ostensively defined concept as effectively "so much of this *received stimulus* and so much of that *received stimulus*"? Or are the elementary symbols going to be derived from the repertoire of internal *responses evoked* by the ostensive process?

For the sake of brevity, I will jump straight on to suggest a mechanism on the second principle, without discussing now the reasons that have led me to favour it in preference to the other.[14]

Suppose we have a device which reacts to incoming stimuli by an act of *replication*. At the very simplest level, let us consider one which has an irritable surface and is designed so that, if it is excited at a certain point, its reaction is a hunting motion over the surface with a finger, which eventually elicits a success signal. Call this, if you like, a scratch-response mechanism. It is easy to see that if this stimulus recurs often enough we can devise a self-adjusting statistical mechanism (see Chapter 12), which will increase the probability that on the next arrival of such a stimulus the scratch mechanism will tend to hunt in its neighbourhood. You can see that if any particular irritation is a sufficiently consistent feature of the flux of incoming stimuli, it can come to elicit the successful scratch response by a series of elementary operations between which the transition probabilities are higher than they would have been originally. It has now evolved something that can serve as an internal symbol of any movements of the incoming stimulus, namely, the sequence by which these movements are successfully replicated.

Suppose now that we have several stimuli — say three forming a triangular pattern — and imagine a mechanism whose constant activity is to "doodle" in speculative movement from one to the other — in other words, it is built to respond with self-guided attempts to organize a programme of movement from one to the other. We will equip it with means of determining that it has successfully finished all its scratching. It goes from one stimulus to another until it gets the indication that it has no more scratching to do. If triangular patterns recur with sufficient frequency in its incoming stimuli, then a process of natural selection, which I think one can easily envisage, is all we need invoke in order to make a device that automatically discovers for itself — and internally names — an abstraction. Stimulated by any triangular pattern, the device will find that the same sequence of elementary commands to its scratching machinery (go ahead, turn, go ahead, turn, go ahead) is required to produce a satisfactory internal "match"; so that we could think of this sequence as becoming one of the internal representative *symbols* of the "experience" of this device — its name for "triangularity". Out of the welter of all possible combinations, this one has acquired the dignity of a symbol for a "universal", through recurring with sufficient frequency among the organizers of successful responses to the flux of incoming stimuli.

One can go on from this to think of *any* incoming pattern which is sufficiently recurrent, or which persists for long enough at a given time to evoke internal matching activity, as gaining for itself the status of a "universal" in the world of discourse of such a device. What we have been doing is to go *behind* the problem of devising a mechanism for *deductive* reasoning, which we can take for granted well enough, to the problem of transforming the information carried by incoming sensory stimuli into a symbolic linguistic form suitable for such a mechanism, which takes us to the problem of *inductive* reasoning. Our typical problem is this: how can we ensure that a mechanism presented with, say, a triangle in the field of its optical receptors can always make calculations appropriate to the presence of (i.e. act as if recognizing) triangularity, irrespective of size, shape, or orientation? What I have been describing is one possible way of solving the problem which in detail is hardly realistic as a model of human brain mechanisms; but it illustrates a principle which I think we should not neglect: the representation of a particular universal by a compresence and/or a sequence of the elementary internal acts involved in responding adaptively to it.

PROBABILISTIC ASPECTS

Now we come to the probabilistic aspect. These elementary components will not always recur in association in equal proportions. A complex universal therefore becomes defined not by simply *enumerating* the internal acts which participate in its symbolization, but by enumerating those *plus* the *relative frequencies* with which they have been involved. And here, of course, our information-space comes into its own; because what we have done, in effect, is to define our universal by a vector in a space which is not quantal (at this macroscopic level at any rate), but has the possibility of representing practically continuous gradations or shades of meaning. The meaning of this universal is defined by the *orientation* of the information vector — by the statistical spectrum, if you like — over the elementary acts of response which exemplars of this universal have evoked in the organism in the past.

Questions now arise thick and fast. Clearly, this just takes us past the first step. We have discussed an artificial organism which can recognize pattern in the flux of incoming stimuli — which can abstract from among its received data those relationships whose recurrence or invariance gives them the status of universals. The next step is to consider the possibility of recognizing pattern in the flux of perceived universals — of abstracting from among the evoked acts of symbolic response those higher-order relationships whose recurrence or invariance gives them also the status of universals.

This, I think, is the essence of the making of *hypotheses* — to predicate pattern of a group of abstractions. Can an artificial organism spontaneously formulate useful hypotheses? I think it can, certainly in the sense that we can devise a second-order probabilistic mechanism, analogous to our first, but one in which each individual basic symbol now represents a pattern of first-order symbols. It is evident that we have here the possibility of a *hierarchy of abstraction*; and indeed this hierarchy itself could in turn become the subject of internal discourse; but perhaps I have said enough to indicate the possibilities.

To summarize: our device, working probabilistically, makes its abstractions by a process of natural selection of matching responses. It chooses a means of (internal) response which is invariant with respect to the transformations that leave the abstraction invariant, by a self-guiding process in which the statistical configuration for each attempt is dependent upon the success of the last. Experience elevates the statistical status of certain response sequences, which can then appear as elements in the internal logical vocabulary. Performing second-order abstractions (as in the formation of hypotheses), or even nth order abstractions, is in principle just a repetition of this process at the next level or at a higher level.

This kind of approach to the mechanics of reasoning might, I think, find a place for most of the concepts that we arrive at from the other direction. Consciousness, for example — if I dare stick my neck out — might be introduced in this way: We might say that the point or area "of conscious attention" in a field of data is the point or area under active internal symbolic replication, or evocative of internal matching response. When a man speaks to another man, the meaning of what he says is defined by a spectrum over the elementary acts of internal response which can be evoked in the hearer. If the hearer is such that when the speaker raises his eyebrows, something inside the hearer happens which corresponds to imitation — the internal initiation of part of the sequence that would normally lead to the raising of eyebrows, and so on — then, clearly, the *meaning* of what the speaker says can be fully represented only in terms of the full basic-symbol complex defined by all the elementary responses evoked. These may include visceral responses and hormonal secretions and what have you. So, along these lines, I think one would say that an organism probably includes in its elementary conceptual alphabet (its catalogue of basic symbols) all the elementary internal acts of response to the environment which have acquired a sufficiently high probabilistic status, and not merely those for which verbal projections have been found.

Without here going into further detail, I should perhaps point out that many human characteristics such as bias, prejudice, preference and the like would have obvious analogues in such a mechanism, in the shape of alterations of the thresholds of excitation or, if you like, distortion of the probability amplitudes, associated with the basic vector components affected by the "bias".

Indeed, along these lines, I think one could go a long way towards simulating what appears to be the ordinary conscious behaviour of human beings. On the other hand, if one were to ask whether such a mechanism could ever be built, I would take refuge for the moment in the blessed phrase "in principle", and say that *in principle* I see no reason why it shouldn't. But I would not myself be surprised, were one to attempt to devise a probabilistic mechanism with the same mobility and other capacities as *homo sapiens*, if one would have to go in for mechanisms in protoplasm instead of mechanisms in copper. That seems to me to be one implication of some of the very neat tricks that we find in the central nervous system.

POSTSCRIPT

The emphasis above on spontaneous activity may need some comment. In the formalism of wave mechanics the notion of probability (of a single event) shades over into that of frequency (of spontaneous occurrence of events) at high wave amplitudes. Thus spontaneous activity can be thought of as the limiting case of increasing probability of activity — as, for example, in a neurone whose threshold is steadily lowered. The suggestion was not that the mechanism should operate on a purely random basis (like proverbial monkeys on a typewriter), but rather that the statistical pattern of its explorations should reflect the "metrical" aspect of the available information. An important feature of such a mechanism would be its ability, unlike Buridan's ass, to act in the absence of adequate information; but any available information of high metron-content would of course be fully used in shaping its exploratory activity.

What I wanted to stress was the readiness with which a spontaneously active mechanism on these lines could evolve categories of description beyond those built into its design, in response to redundancy in the pattern of demand from the environment.

The passing reference to "conscious awareness" I would now want to extend and qualify in several respects (see, for example, Ref. 25); but the essential suggestion stands, that the correlate of awareness should be sought in an internal adaptive matching response, rather than in the mere arrival of sensory stimulation at a particular internal point.

CHAPTER 6

Operational Aspects of Some Fundamental Concepts of Human Communication*

In everyday language we are accustomed to speak of the *meaning* and the *relevance* of information. In the statistical theory of communication,†[31] on the other hand, no such concepts appear. Indeed its founders have very properly insisted that the "amount of information" (or, better, the selective information-content) of a signal, as they define it, bears no direct relation to the semantic function of the signal.

From its inception, naturally, the theory has been plagued by questions of the relationship of its concepts to those normally associated with the term information. Where do concepts like meaning fit into the picture? Or is it that the concept of information which the communication engineer has in mind is a quite different one from the concept of the semanticists?

The trouble here appears to be due largely to a confusion of the concept of *information* with that of *information-content* — the confusion of a *thing* with a *measure* of a thing. Communication engineers have not developed a concept of information at all.

* A paper given at the 9th International Conference on Significs, Amersfoort (Netherlands), 1953. First published in *Synthese*, 9, 1954, pp. 182–98.

† Referred to by some as Information Theory, but never so by Shannon, its chief originator. Information Theory logically embraces a much wider field.

They have developed a theory dealing explicitly with only one particular feature or aspect of messages "carrying" information — their unexpectedness or surprise value. Unexpectedness is a feature not only of messages but of other things, such as the states of a physical system, as well. Physicists had already developed a quantitative method of measuring unexpectedness by Boltzmann's statistical concept of entropy. What Shannon and others did was to adapt and extend this method to the measurement of the unexpectedness of messages. Their measure of unexpectedness, the average logarithm of the improbability of the message, $-\sum p_i \log p_i$, is not therefore *information* but simply a particular measure of what they termed *amount-of-information*: (i.e.) *the minuteness* of the selection which the message makes from the set or "ensemble" of all possible messages.*

Semanticists on the other hand are concerned with different features of information, such as its logical complexity and its meaning. But both engineers and semanticists have in mind the same concept of information, in the sense that we can find one definition of the term which will cover all its uses. Both mean by information that which promotes or validates representational activity (activity from which it is possible to infer something about some other state of affairs). Both are entitled to regard the function of information as to be selective: to prescribe *choice* or *decision*. The engineer seeks to define a suitable measure of the unexpectedness or infrequency of the choice, and calls his measure the selective information-content. The semanticist may seek to define suitable measures of the logical complexity of the representational activity evoked, and is also entitled to call these "measures of information-content", in various complementary

* In this ensemble the different possible messages are pictured as occupying space proportional to their relative probabilities, so that the least-probable message occupies the smallest space and requires the most minute selective operation. But the technicalities do not here concern us.

senses. It is a mere solecism, however, to regard the concept of information itself as identical to any of these measures; to do so, besides being grammatically absurd, leads inevitably to debate over spurious paradoxes, which it is part of our present aim to resolve.

So much then for clearing the ground. The view I have offered is that while the connection between statistical and semantic features of information cannot but be indirect, these are features of one and the same central concept, which admits of a single universally applicable operational definition. Our aim must now be to elucidate the connection by exploring the basis of this operational definition.

On what does information operate? Ultimately, we say, "on the receiver's mind". At once we are nervous of losing ourselves — and our respectability! — in a morass of subjective terminology. Cannot we put it differently? Cannot we find an objective description in "observer-language" of what goes on when a man receives information? If we could, then it might be possible to form a coherent picture of the whole process of communication, in which concepts like selective information-content and concepts like meaning would both find a place, and be seen in their proper relationship.

Here I can attempt only an outline of the possibilities, amounting to little more than a programme. It may however suffice to indicate more clearly the scope — and the degree of overlap — of the concepts used in the two fields.

THE SUBJECTIVE ASPECT

Our first precaution must be to distinguish clearly between the two complementary languages in which we may describe an activity like gaining information. There is first (*a*) the private *actor-language* in which I as actor describe what I mean by my knowing something; secondly (*b*) there is the public *observer-language* in which we might hope that a super-mechanic of the brain could describe what goes on in the human organism as the correlate of my actor-account.

There seems to be no good reason to miss any clues we can gain from the use of words from both languages, provided we avoid the common pitfall of careless mixing of the two. As far as possible we shall carry on our discussion in discrete stages, each consistently using one language or the other. It will be fruitful to develop the two descriptions in parallel, since each can be suggestive of questions to be explored in the other. On the other hand, we shall be wise not to presume the existence of any simple one-to-one correspondence, but to treat what correspondence we find as permissive rather than confirmatory.

Let us then begin in subjective actor-language, where our feeling for the notion of information is clearest and our thinking perhaps woolliest. I normally say I have gained information when I know something now that I didn't know before: when *what I know* has changed.

How much more information do I gain from one statement, or experiment, than from another? I might be able to answer this question quantitatively if I could *measure* the corresponding changes in what I know. I get more information from that which makes a bigger change in what I know.

How could we hope to measure — or even to define quantitatively — changes in what I know? Could we perhaps count the minimum number of independent simple sentences in which I could describe the change? If our sentences were all independent, ideal, "atomic" sentences in the logician's sense, this might do for one kind of measure. But the difficult problem is not so much to define appropriate measures when we are given the ideal language, but to discipline real language into a form sufficiently "atomic" for our purpose.

Scientific language is one of the few that lend of themselves readily to such discipline, and in an early paper[12] the author suggested definitions of two complementary measures of the "semantic information content" of scientific statements, based on their appeal to the inherently quantal processes of measurement and verification. In the vector-representation suggested in that paper, the *meaning* and *relevance* of scientific information had especially simple geometrical correlates. But scientific language is too easily quantified to be typical; and although the work was catalytic in the development of the present line of approach, no familiarity with it is necessary in what follows.*

---

* It may also be mentioned that the author's work on semantic measures of scientific information, first described in a lecture in January 1948, was initiated some years before the publication of Shannon's papers and is concerned to answer quite different questions from a different starting-point. Misunderstanding has sometimes arisen from attempts to see it as an application or extension of communication theory. The relation of the two has been discussed in an earlier paper. (See Appendix).

For we are here concerned with information in general; and normal human language is notoriously different from the ideal of the scientist or the logician. Am I sure, moreover, that I can always fully describe all changes in my state of knowledge in sentences, or indeed in any objective symbolisation? Is what I know limited to what I can describe? For a starting-point that begs no such questions we must move a stage farther back.

THE OPERATIONAL EFFECT OF INFORMATION

Let us do so by asking in more general, operational terms what difference it makes when I gain information. Fundamentally it implies that in some circumstance or other my *expectations* will be different. I am now conditionally *ready to react differently*. The reactions potentially affected may be internal or external. They may themselves take the form of choices from among a number of possible later states of readiness to react, choices which will now be different as a result of my gaining information. It is the hierarchy of such readinesses — my total state of readiness for adaptive or goal-directed activity — which changes when I gain information. Information in fact could be defined in actor-language as that which alters my total state of adaptive readiness in this sense.

If I were a simple sort of being with only a clear-cut set of independent states of readiness (analogous to the states of readiness represented by the possible settings of independent levers in a railway signal-box), then it would be possible in principle to measure the amount of information I receive in terms of the number of elementary decisions (analogous to the number of changes in lever-settings) evoked in response to it. As we shall see later, some sort of equivalent measure can be defined for the much more complex type of organism that we appear to be.

In parentheses at this point it may be wise to guard against a possible pitfall. Our language might suggest that we picture my gaining information in actor-language as a two-stage activity: first my conscious receipt of information, then my response to it. This however would be a misinterpretation. Our suggestion is that the act of perception is *constituted* by the act of successful internal adaptive response, not that it evokes it as a sequel.

It is not denied that in observer-language we can distinguish two stages. Of all the objects in the field of vision, for example, only a few are normally perceived at any one time — those that have "caught the attention" as we say. Stimuli corresponding to the presence of the others are *received*; but they evoke no "matching-response"[14,15] in the organism — at least none structured to correspond to the individual objects. These objects are not *per*ceived.

Our suggestion is simply that of the two stages that can be described in observer-language, only the second finds a correlate in actor-language: in effect, that the activity of knowing *is* an activity of (internal) adaptive response.

It is sometimes suggested that the activity of knowing amounts to the gradual construction of a mental model of the external world. Information might then be defined as that which adds something to our model, either introducing new features or increasing our confidence in the old.

There is a sense in which this description is defensible. Our suggestion however will be that what is internally imitated is not a static structure of relations between *things*, so much as the dynamic structure of relations between *events*. *Events* of perception are what we know primarily, and what is organised as we receive information is our conditional readiness to match the pattern of events of perception by the pattern of our own internal or external reaction. The basic symbols in which our "model" of the world could most economically be described would stand, not for objects in the world, but for characteristic patterns in the events of perception. These events themselves, be it remembered, we have taken to be acts of internal adaptive response.

In the concept of the total state of readiness we have a possible bridge between actor- and observer-language. We must first remark that our state of readiness differs from that of a signal-box primarily in that it does not prescribe all our reactions *uniquely*. In many cases in which our information is incomplete there may be several possible adaptive reactions equally reasonable on the evidence we have.*

In any event, it would seem that the closest correlate of my state of readiness in observer-language is a specification of a stochastic rather than a deterministic process (see Chapter 5). Of course, a catalogue of probabilities and conditional probabilities is not what I *mean* by my state of readiness. But the latter in theory would presumably reveal itself (if only it were sufficiently stationary, which in practice it is not) through the statistical structure of my total adaptive reaction-pattern; and I should not be able to defend a purported description of my total state of readiness which was inconsistent with the observed structure.†

Remembering then that the total reaction-pattern includes internal as well as external activity, we shall take as the objective correlate of my total state of readiness the matrix of transition-probabilities or transition-probability-matrix (t.p.m.) describing statistically the total adaptive reaction-pattern to all possible configurations of stimuli, internal and external. Our aim is not of course to define this as *observable*. Like any non-stationary probability, the probabilities in the t.p.m. can be interpreted only as frequencies in an ensemble of identical organisms, and not as frequencies in the time-series of a given organism.

We shall see below that the t.p.m. may have a physical determinant that is in principle perfectly observable; but observability does not need to worry us. Our aim is simply to

---

* Retrospectively, it is conventional to find a "cause" for our ultimate choice in such cases, but in many it is doubtful whether such phrases as "the whim of the moment" describe a cause or its absence.

† Comparisons of this sort are of course what we use to detect hypocrisy, the non-stationary character of the state of readiness and the absence of data on internal activity being ignored to the detriment of justice as well as charity!

define conceptually an objective correlate of the subjective notion of my state of readiness in terms of which we have so far defined the concept of information. Our suggestion is that by discussing the effect of information on the t.p.m., we can find a place for all the concepts clustering round the notion of information in both communication theory and semantics — at least for their correlates in observer-language, which is perhaps as much as an objective theory can hope to do.

It will be helpful to begin by summarising the evidence for the statistical picture of the ultimate receiver of information, in terms of which we shall frame our definitions.

The Central Nervous System

The central nervous system is a community of some 10^{10} electrically sensitive cells and their fibrous "processes", linked on the one hand with effector organs (limbs, glands, etc.) which have fields of activity both external and internal, and on the other with receptor organs (eyes, muscle-spindles, etc.) both external and internal.

A typical cell can be "excited" to send an electrical impulse down one of its efferent fibres as a result of electrical and/or chemical changes in its neighbourhood. The size of the impulse is substantially independent of the nature of the change that evoked it. The readiness with which cells can be excited may be increased or decreased by:

(*a*) general factors governing the metabolism of most or all the population;

(*b*) specific agents rendering some group of cells more and others less active or sensitive;

(*c*) electrical and chemical activity in the neighbourhood insufficient in itself to excite impulses;

(*d*) changes in geometry of the system such as growth in the length or diameter of fibres, constriction of blood vessels, and the like.

It cannot be too strongly stressed that a description of the system is not completed by saying which cells are "wired" to which, and which cells are active at a given instant; nor is the number of degrees of freedom of the system determined by counting the number of cells. It is true that each cell must be in one of two states: excited or unexcited; but many cells have dozens or hundreds of fibrous processes ramifying over an effective volume much greater than that of the cell body, and each making perhaps hundreds of approaches within critical distance of other fibres and cell bodies. The readiness with which the cell can be excited is a continuously-variable parameter — or a number of parameters — depending among other things on the geometry of the whole ramification and its chemical state. The delay in response (of the order of 1 millisecond) is yet another variable of importance (see below). The total number of degrees of freedom may therefore average out at many more than one per cell.*

As some small consolation for the would-be model-maker, large groups of cells often appear to be so interlocked as to function as co-operative units. The effective number of *functional* degrees of freedom is therefore probably many orders of magnitude smaller than the dimensionality of the total description.

Some cells are spontaneously active. Others are highly resistant to stimulation, requiring many impulses to converge on them simultaneously before they will "fire". We express this by saying that the "height of the threshold to stimulation" varies from one cell to another. The higher the threshold, the lower the probability that a given impulse will excite the cell. "Effective height of threshold" (depending on the factors outlined above among others) thus can be thought of as the physical determinant of *improbability of excitation*. An "effective height of threshold" can be defined separately for each fibre converging on a given cell.

The strength of a stimulus is often represented by the repetition frequency of a continuous train of impulses in a

---

* Calculations of the limit to memory capacity on the basis of 1 unit of information per cell are thus unrealistic, even if cells were assumed to be invariable units, which they are not.

single fibre. This together with the foregoing evidence gives strong encouragement to consider a model of the nervous system in which the significant variables are the *thresholds* of the various elements, in the general sense which we have given the term. We should then have the following correlation:

Strong stimulus:	high frequency of impulses
Weaker stimulus:	lower frequency of impulses
Still weaker stimulus:	corresponding probability of a single impulse in a given time-interval

As intensity diminishes, we pass from speaking in terms of frequency of impulses to speaking in terms of the probability of a single impulse, in the same way as we do in the photon-description of the intensity of light. The parallel is suggestive, but need not detain us now.

There are any number of potential models in electronic "relaxation oscillators" which (given the presence of a finite random noise level) show the same smooth transition as their applied bias is reduced.

Four phenomena should be mentioned which may have relevance to the problems of short-term and/or long-term memory: the first is that of *adaptation*, whereby the threshold in many cases rises with time (the frequency drops) if the stimulus is maintained. It normally recovers after a short time.

The second is that of *facilitation*, whereby the transfer of a signal at a given point from one cell to another may increase the sensitivity (lower the threshold) to excitation there at a later time.

The third which might conceivably be relevant is that of "potentiation". A fibre which has been saturated by excessive stimulation is found to deliver abnormally large impulses for a short time after recovery. These are correspondingly more effective than usual in stimulating other cells.

The fourth is the differential change in diameter of some fibres with use. It is not known how general this may be, but if it occurs centrally it may have great importance. The reason is that the speed of transmission in a fibre depends on its diameter. Now the probability of excitation of a cell is often critically sensitive to the relative *timing* of two or more impulses convergent on it. A change of as little as $\frac{1}{10}$ millisecond[10] may alter the probability from almost zero to almost unity. The change in temporal relationships with use might well provide us with just the threshold-control mechanism required to account for learning and memory.

But we can afford for our present purpose to wait and see. The point is that when we think of the whole system, a population in continuous electrical and micro-chemical activity, we have abundant evidence for a model in which the probability of transition from one state of excitation to each of the other possible following states can be modified by any number of continuously variable factors in combination, of which perhaps the most flexible and subtle is the pattern of temporal relationships between impulses. Minute changes of delay in transmission (not necessarily through variation in diameter of fibres — see above) can drastically modify the whole structure of the activity of the population. In addition, whole areas can be depressed or activated by general chemical or electrical agents.

THE PHYSICAL REPRESENTATION OF THE PERCEIVED WORLD

Unfortunately we are still probably many years away from understanding properly in these terms what goes on when a man receives information. We can follow some signals a little way into his head, but they soon lose themselves in a scurry of activity that we are at a loss to interpret.

But our survey has been some guide as to the kind of model of the process mediating perception that may not be unrealistic, and will serve as a peg to which to anchor our later discussion. For our limited purpose we can ignore much of the detail that is obscure.

The essential notion around which we shall build our concept of perceptual activity is that of *adaptive* or *matching-response*. Any mechanism such as we have described, subjected to a flow of signals through its receptors, is likely to be stimulated to all kinds of internal or external activity. What then particularly characterises activity that we shall call adaptive? How do we distinguish adaptive response from evoked activity in general? Here we can give only a summary answer. The question has been much discussed, and the author has dealt with it in detail in Refs. 14 and 15. The basic requirements are two:

(*a*) In the organism there should be one or more *evaluatory mechanisms* embodying criteria of success or failure: mechanisms, that is, emitting signals indicating the difference between the present state of the organism and some acceptable condition or goal-state.

(*b*) Then (the crucial feature) these signals must be allowed to alter the controls that govern activity (including the choice of subsidiary goals if necessary) in such a way as to reduce (at least statistically) the difference between the present state and the goal-state. Evidently the controls can come to rest only if the goal-state is attained and the difference-signal reads "zero". Unless this is so they should always be found actively opposing any changes in the state of affairs which would tend to increase the difference-reading. An adaptive or matching-response is one which is goal-directed in this way towards minimising the degree of mismatch as indicated by evaluatory mechanisms. We might define it as "activity under the correction of evaluatory signals".

This is of course the type of control familiar in engineering under the name of negative feedback. The standard illustration is the thermostat, in which the degree of mismatch between the present temperature and an adjustable prescribed temperature is evaluated by a simple device which turns heat on or off as required to reduce the degree of mismatch. If the prescribed temperature is altered the system will (in its own time!) follow the adjustments.

The point of special relevance here is that insofar as an adaptive response is successful, the automatic movements of the goal-directed control-centre will in quite a precise sense *mirror* the current state of affairs, or rather those features of the state of affairs to which it is responding adaptively. The state of the control-centre is in effect a *representation* of those features of the state of affairs, just as much as a code-pattern of binary symbols could be. In each case we need a principle of interpretation, provided in one case by knowledge of the evaluatory criteria, in the other by the code book. In each case, given these, we can infer certain things about the state of affairs represented.

Let us now generalise. It is perhaps obvious that when I move my finger to follow the outline of a moving spot of light, the configuration of the thresholds of the nervous system controlling my muscle-movements is an implicit representation of the position of the spot. But what about listening to something, or looking at something?

Our suggestion is that here also perception is distinguished from reception by the element of adaptive response: that in perception an internal pattern of activity is evoked (under evaluatory correction) which in some sense (we do not know what) *matches* the spatio-temporal rhythm of incoming signals from ear or eye. Once again, if this is so, the controlling threshold-configuration (or of course the activity it determines) may be considered as a representation of current events perceived.

In short, our suggestion is that whenever information is received, there is in the human organism adaptive activity; and that the current changes in the "setting of the controls" (the threshold configuration) that lead to a satisfactory matching-response (relative to definite though not necessarily permanent criteria) form a representation of the information actually perceived — i.e. what the man is noticing in the flux of events.*

Such activity will be selective and abstractive — as human perception notoriously is. Any adaptive activity, producing internal spatio-temporal rhythms that are a good enough "match" within the resolving-power of the evaluatory mechanism, will pass muster. In many cases more than one such response could meet the criteria, and the control mechanism might fluctuate between two or more adaptive states. This may plausibly be the basis of many ambiguities of visual perception, such as the familiar isometric drawing of a cube which appears in either of two aspects. It would also seem to account satisfactorily for some classical optical illusions.

So far we have not discussed the way in which evaluative correction could be applied. At one extreme we could envisage a logical network which computed the best correction to minimise the mismatch. At the other we might envisage undisciplined trial and error by random alteration of thresholds until success was signalled. This would be slow to converge, and indeed convergence could not be guaranteed. Let us suppose however that we have a hierarchy of mechanisms for altering the *relative probabilities* of trial of mechanisms for altering the relative probabilities ... to as many terms as we wish. If now we use our logical network to preselect the areas of trial, and use evaluatory signals to lower all thresholds associated with successful trials and raise all associated with failures, it is evident that any statistical regularities in the flux of events will tend to find themselves reflected sooner or later in the relative probabilities of trials.

* The Kantian categories here find their physical embodiment not in the nature of a set of built-in *filters*, but in the characteristics of the possible modes of *response*, partly built-in, partly evolved. In actor-language, my world (as known) is structured for me in terms of my basic modes of matching myself to it. I know only those features of the world of events that stir me to adapt myself to match them; and the form of my knowing is determined by the form of adaptation in which I find myself matched to them.

Such a hierarchical mechanism could in time come to represent a set of abstractions from the statistical structure of events to which the organism has made adaptive response, even with only the roughest guidance from its logical analysers. These abstractions would in fact amount to hypotheses about the world of events, representing implicitly what past experience has shown to be its steady features.

The higher-order probabilities in such a system will tend to change more slowly, the lower-order most rapidly. Changes in the lower which persist in occurring will tend to become reflected in changes at a higher level adapted to evoke the lower changes automatically. Thus gradually only those aspects of situations which are *new* to the organism will come to evoke adaptive activity at the level of the controlling mechanisms. (In actor-language, familiar items will come to be expected, and will yield a smaller and smaller amount of information. They may even cease to be noticed.)

But this is not the place for a full discussion of the theory of learning and memory that could be based on our conceptual model. It will suffice if we have gained a clear picture of what is meant by the hierarchy of threshold-configurations governing adaptive response. For this in quite a literal sense determines the state of conditional readiness of the organism for adaptive response. Corresponding to a given threshold-configuration there will be a hierarchy of transition-probabilities — the t.p.m. — which we regard as the correlate in observer-language of my state of readiness. We can now complete our transition from the subjective discussion of information. Information can be generally defined as that which promotes or validates representational activity. In the human organism this activity is a change in the t.p.m. that specifies adaptive response and the hierarchy of conditional readinesses for adaptive response.*

* It should be remembered that only the adaptive t.p.m., and not the t.p.m. for all activity, embodies the representation of the perceived world.

MEANING

We are now in a position to define (at least conceptually) objective correlates for the notions of the meaning and relevance of information. The *meaning* of a signal to a given receiver (in observer-language) may be defined as the selective operation which the signal defines (in a logical, not a physical sense) on the set of possible states of readiness (i.e. of the t.p.m.). The *selective information-content* for the receiver as defined in communication theory is a logarithmic measure of the unexpectedness of that selective operation. Thus we can readily see why even to the receiver the selective information-content is not directly related to the meaning. If the state of readiness happened already to match the signal, this would imply that the prior probability of adaptive response was unity and the selective information-content nil. The meaning however is unaltered.

Has the notion of meaning any quantitative aspects? Subjectively we sometimes speak as if it had. We have an intuitive notion of "richness" of meaning, as the opposite of simplicity. It would seem reasonable to identify this with the *complexity* of the selective operation (or of the features of the state of readiness organised by it). If we like we may carry the mathematical representation a stage further. Assuming that the degrees of freedom of the mechanism controlling the t.p.m. are finite in number, we can represent a particular adaptive modification conveniently by a point in a multi-dimensional space of the same number of dimensions, or by the vector linking that point to the origin. This space, which we may term "response-space", in effect represents the universe of discourse for the organism, since all information received may be (indeed on our definition must be) represented by the motion of a point within it. Its dimensionality defines the number of independent symbols that could be necessary and sufficient for the complete exchange of such information;* but since the probability of occupancy of much of the space will be negligible, a sufficient working vocabulary of basic symbols could be much smaller.

This picture offers a symbolic representation of the meaning of a signal by the *orientation* of the vector describing its selective operation. Our notion of "richness of meaning" may then find an adequate definition as the number of dimensions of the subspace "spanned" by the vector: the number of its components.

Unfortunately the picture is misleading in one important respect, for the degrees of freedom of the control system may themselves be liable to adaptive trial and error like everything else. Thus the identification of the basic vectors is not permanent. The dimensionality and metric of response-space itself will change with experience — even in the process of communication. The picture can serve only as a basis for our definition of the meaning to the receiver at time of receipt.

A distinction should be carefully made between the notion of meaning-to-the-receiver, which we have here defined, and the notions of intended-meaning and generally-accepted-meaning. Analogous definitions of these other concepts are obvious. In each the essential notion is formally the selective function (intended, effected, etc.) on a set of possible responses.

We may assume that part of the human mechanism of adaptive response governs a variety of internal activities such as humoral secretion and the like, which are not directly coupled to our mechanisms for handling propositions and are only vaguely describable in actor-language if at all. The nature and extent of such activity or readiness for it could be expected however to make a difference to the quality of awareness. It is represented in response-space by component-

---

* This assumes that each symbol could be qualified by a continuously variable parameter. The number of two valued symbols required would of course be greater.

vectors on the same footing *a priori* as any others. If this is so it may serve as a further caution against supposing that the meaning of a message can be exhausted by a catalogue of its equivalent propositional content. Both the intended meaning and the understood meaning in our sense of the term may have non-propositional components, without being rendered in the least indefinite in consequence. It seems important to free ourselves from the notion that something *is* indefinite unless someone can *talk* definitely about it.

So far we have been concerned only with the meaning of a complete message: i.e. something designed to evoke a definite selection from the set of possible responses. A single word of a message does not in general evoke a unique selective operation. It may be thought of as setting up a conditional probability-distribution over possible matching-responses, which is gradually moulded and narrowed down as the message is completed. The meaning of a word can thus be represented not by a point but by a distribution in response-space.

RELEVANCE

What of the concept of relevance? We say that information has more relevance to one question than to another. It is necessary first therefore to consider how a *question* is represented in our formalism.

Receiving the answer to a question determines a subset of adaptive responses, which until then were undetermined or only partly determined (i.e. statistically). To frame a question is to specify this subset of undetermined responses — or in our formalism, the corresponding subspace of response-space. It is to invite a selective operation on this subspace.

The notion of the relevance of information to a question is thus linked with the notion of the proportion of the total selective operation that concerns the required sub-space.

It is tempting to seek a metric for response-space such that (as in the formalism of scientific information theory) a given question could be represented by a particular ray in the space, and the relevance of information defined as a number between 0 and 1, represented by the cosine (or better, the square of the cosine) of the angle between the information-vector and that ray. This would ensure that a selective operation on precisely the subspace specified by the question could have a relevance of unity, while a selective operation on an orthogonal subspace (related to none of the readinesses specified by the question) would have a relevance of zero. With such a metric the square of the length of the information-vector could serve as a further quantitative measure of information-content, being additive for the combination of information-vectors.

But this must form part of a later programme. For the moment we may be content that within this same objective framework there is evidently room for a quantitative concept of relevance, as some conventional measure of overlap between the selective operation performed on response-space by information, and the selective operation invited by the question to which its relevance is to be estimated.

It may be noted that "irrelevant information", which operates on a subspace orthogonal to that specified by the question, is clearly distinct from "semantic noise", which (is any feature of a message that) reduces the sharpness of a selective operation on the required subspace.

THE COMMUNICATION PROCESS

By way of summary, we may now review the picture of the communication process which we have been building up.

The object of communication in actor-language is to evoke in the mind of the receiver something which the originator has in mind. We have taken as the correlate of "having in mind" in observer-language the possession of a certain objective state of conditional readiness for internal and external adaptive activity.* The problem of communication is thus in observer-language the problem of evoking in the receiver a state of readiness in some desired respects similar to that of the originator.

It would be tedious to give an observer-description of the whole process whereby physical symbols are conventionally associated with appropriate states of readiness. Engineering communication theory is concerned with the transmission process by which a symbol chosen by the originator is caused to appear before the receiver.

In its most economical form this uses physical signals not to *depict* but to *select* a standard representation of the symbol at the receiving end. The communication engineer measures the selective information-content of such signals, not in terms of the selective operation performed by the symbol on the ensemble of states of readiness of the human receiver, but in terms of the selective operation performed by the signal on the ensemble of symbols. The symbols are represented in this ensemble in the proportions in which they normally occur, the most frequently used occupying the largest space and being most easily selected.

The ensemble of states of readiness of the receiving human being may have quite different proportions, unless he were the only user of the communication channel and had an ideal matching-response mechanism.

It should therefore be clear why the selective information-content estimated by the engineer and the selective information-content estimated by the receiver are numerically different quantities, though the concepts denoted by the term are one and the same. Selective information-content in fact measures not a *stuff*, but a *relation* (selective power) between a signal and an ensemble. Confusion would often be avoided

---

* This may include, e.g. the states of half-readiness correlated with what we call imagining something, where some of our readinesses are organised "as if" it were the case, others are suppressed. See Refs. 14 and 15.

and debate dissolved if the ensemble were defined with every estimate.

As a final illustration of this approach we might consider the familiar conundrum: Is information multiplied when a newspaper is printed? Information being that which promotes representational activity, it seems fair to say that it is. But what is often meant by the question is rather: "Is selective information-content multiplied when we produce fresh copies of the same newspaper?"

To this the obvious response is to ask "relative to what ensemble?". If the ensemble is that of all possible newspaper contents, it is clear that the production of fresh copies in no way affects the selective operation performed on this ensemble, unless successive copies were liable to random errors so that fresh copies enabled the selective operation to be statistically more precise.

So there is no paradox. It was only a solecism.

CONCLUSION

Our discussion of communication has suggested that

(*a*) there is but one concept of information, though there are several complementary concepts of information-content; there is no specifically engineering concept of *information*;

(*b*) the concept of the meaning of a message can be operationally defined as its selective function in relation to the "adaptive-response-space" of the human receiver;

(*c*) the prior improbability of the adaptive response evoked defines logarithmically the selective information-content for the receiver in the same way that the prior improbability of the symbol evoking the response does for the communication engineer;

(*d*) these improbabilities being measured from different ensembles, there is no reason for the receiver's estimate of selective information-content and the engineer's estimate to have the same numerical value, though the concepts are the same;

(e) selective information-content in fact measures not a stuff but a relation, and is not defined unless both terminals of the relation are specified;

(f) concepts such as the relevance of a message find ready correlates in terms of the function of the message on the adaptive-response-space of the receiver;

(g) to identify the dimensions of adaptive-response-space should enable the definition of an ideally economical language; but unfortunately the variation from one individual to another and in one individual from time to time render any hope of a completely unambiguous universal language illusory in principle.

POSTSCRIPT

It will be evident that this operational approach to semantics was closely connected with other ideas about the nature and organisation of mind-like behaviour in general, and human behaviour in particular. These were sketched in a series of papers (from 1949 onwards) to be published as a separate volume. Their central notion was that the organisation of intelligent agency required the field of action to be represented internally, in terms of the constraints imposed by its structure upon the transition-probabilities (the conditional probabilities of various possible next steps in various given circumstances) governing the planning of any action that must take account of that structure. A structured environment implies some degree of redundancy or predictability in the sequence of actions, internal and external, demanded by it; and this in turn suggested that redundant features of the control sequence could be internally preorganised to increase efficiency. The internal hierarchic "organising system" needed to mould the conditional probabilities of action in this way was thought of as constituting ipso facto the necessary internal representation of the world, and hence the ultimate "target" for any indicative communications from another organism.

It should perhaps be emphasised that the meaning of a message is not here defined as the effect it produces in the recipient. The meaning it has for a given recipient is a logical property, which it possesses whether or not it has a chance to exercise its function on the recipient. The definition of meaning in the original paper as "the selective operation which the signal performs on the set of possible states of readiness" was open to misinterpretation on this score, since it was easy to confuse the logical operation on the set with the physical operation on the organism. To avoid this misunderstanding I have made some changes in wording in the present version.

CHAPTER 7

The Place of 'Meaning' in the Theory of Information*

FOREWORD

By the time of our Third London Symposium on Information Theory in 1955, it had become something of an accepted saying that 'information theory has nothing to do with meaning'. The time seemed ripe to question this hardening dogma, and the following paper to some extent overlaps with earlier chapters in its attempt to do so constructively.

Some comments in discussion of Professor Yngve's paper in the same symposium have been worked into the present text for convenience, in the paragraph headed 'Mechanical Translation'.

INTRODUCTION

It is now† seven years since Shannon published his papers on a 'Mathematical Theory of Communication'.[31,36] In this he defined a quantity which he called 'amount-of-information', which is essentially a logarithmic measure of the statistical unexpectedness (reciprocal of probability) of the message concerned. Since the unexpectedness of a message need have no direct connection with its semantic content or meaning, Shannon wisely insisted that the concept of 'meaning' was outside the scope of his theory.

This innocent statement by Shannon has given rise to two unfortunate consequences.

---

* *'Information Theory'* (E. C. Cherry, ed.), Butterworths, 215–25, 1956

† 1955

In the first place the original sense of Shannon's warning has sometimes been forgotten and he is credited with the view that the whole theory of information (which includes his own theory of the unexpectedness of information as a vital part) has nothing to do with 'meaning'.

Secondly, and largely in consequence of this, the idea has become current that the whole subject of meaning is not satisfactory for the information theorist. 'Subjective', 'vague', 'dangerous', are the adjectives with which it is often smothered.

Now there is no doubt that the idea of 'meaning' has subjective aspects, that it is vague in many people's minds, and that it still in fact provokes debate among philosophers of the subject: it is at least as 'dangerous' in these respects as the idea of 'information' itself. But it is no more so; and in this paper I venture to outline a tentative account of the place of 'meaning' in the theory of information which I hope, though dealing by definition with the human subject, may be objective, precise and (sufficiently) safe.

The Theory of Information

It must be understood that if anyone wishes to use the term 'theory of information' exclusively for Shannon's statistical theory of communication he cannot of course be prevented, but he must then realize that we are here discussing something wider for which he must coin his own name. By the theory of information we shall mean broadly the theory of processes by which representations come into being, together with the theory of those abstract features which are common to a representation and that which it represents. By a representation of X we shall mean a set of events or objects exhibiting in at least one respect (even if only statistically) the pattern of relationships between the components of the situation X. By information we shall mean that which justifies representational activity: that to which logical appeal is made to justify a representation.

Information that the water-level at Richmond is 10 ft., for example, logically justifies a representation of the water-level at Richmond as 10 ft. Whether the information is true or false is another matter. If it is true the representation corresponds with the actual state of affairs at Richmond; if not, it corresponds with a fictitious state of affairs. The information is what was essential to justify the making of a representation at all.

So far our definitions have been qualitative. They have been framed so as to apply to a wide range, if not all, of the common uses of the term information, including those of communication theorists. When we come to quantitative measures, it is essential, as Shannon has pointed out,[34] to distinguish the qualitative concept of *information* from the various quantitative measures of *amount-of-information* of which Shannon's is one.

As a basic definition of amount-of-information or information-content it is reasonable (in view of our definition of information as that which justifies representational activity) to take 'an additive measure of the equivalent number of elementary steps or stages in the representational activity justified'. This has the merit of covering all three measures of information-content so far found useful.

(*a*) Shannon's measure indicates the minimum equivalent number of binary steps by which the representation concerned may be selected from an ensemble of possible representations. This has suggested the term 'selective-information-content' for Shannon's measure of 'amount-of-information'.

(*b*) The two complementary measures of what we may term 'descriptive-information-content' indicate the equivalent number of elementary steps or stages by which the representation concerned may be constructed: (i) the 'structural-information-content' or 'logon-content' indicates the minimum equivalent number of independent features which must be specified — the number of degrees of freedom or logical dimensionality of the representation; (ii) the 'metrical-information-content' or 'metron-content' indicates the equivalent number of units of evidence which the information provides for the construction of the representation (e.g. the number of minimally significant events, in the case of a scientific representation of an experimental result).

In 1952 Bar-Hillel and Carnap[1] (hereafter referred to as B and C) suggested two possible measures of the information-content of statements in an artificial language system. Briefly, they consider representations constructed from 'atomic statements', each of which asserts that a particular 'individual' of a finite set has one of a finite set of 'properties'.

In order to derive quantitative measures, however, they consider not the structure of a given representation, but its power to imply possible statements. In particular they consider the large class of statements formed by taking each possible atomic statement or its negation and combining them with the disjunction 'or': for example, '*A*1 or *A*2 or not-*B*1 or ... etc.' These are the weakest possible statements in the language system, and are called 'content-elements'. The class of content-elements logically implied by a given statement is then called its 'content', and is suggested by B and C as an explication of the 'information' conveyed by it. A suitable measure of this class, the 'content-measure', is suggested as one possible explication of the 'amount of information conveyed' in its semantic sense. This measure equals zero if a statement is true and unity if it is false, and may be thought of as the inductive probability of the negation of the statement. Unfortunately it is not additive for independent statements.

Accordingly B and C propose a second measure, the negative log of the inductive probability of the statement itself, which they call the 'measure of information'. This is, of course, additive, and differs from Shannon's familiar measure only in using inductive rather than statistical probability.

A connection can readily be made between this latter approach and that of descriptive information theory (which owing to its origins I called earlier the 'theory of scientific information'). In descriptive information theory we are concerned with the analysis of representations in terms of their logical dimensionality and their weight of evidence. Each dimension or degree of freedom of a representation corresponds to one of B's and C's 'individuals'. To each may be attributed a variable number of indistinguishable 'metrons' representing the 'weight of evidence' or 'number of elementary events' it subsumes. It is generally possible, in any given case, to compute the number of different possible representations. The logarithm of the number (base 2), called 'amount of detail' in reference 12, seems quite close to the 'measure of information' defined by B and C. If the inductive probability of any one representation were inversely proportional to the number of possibilities, the two measures would in fact be the same. In many cases the total metron-content, or the maximum per logon, may be fixed, and if so this will affect the probability distribution and introduce a difference between the two measures. There seems however no reason why the label 'semantic' should not be attached equally to B's and C's measures and to those of logon- and metron-content, and to 'amount of detail'. All are concerned with the structure, rather than merely the rarity, of a representation.

To B's and C's 'content-measure' there corresponds no directly analogous measure of descriptive information-content hitherto defined. Numerically it corresponds to the fraction of the total information-space* which is left unoccupied by the description concerned. Since scientific descriptions are seldom given, and still more seldom accepted, in disjunctive form, the class of sentences considered in my theory of descriptive information was much more restricted, and admits of measurement by simpler parameters.

---

* See first paragraph of section: '*Meaning*' *in the Formalism of Information Theory*, below.

The point at present, however, is that our general definition of information-content applies, additivity apart, to Bar-Hillel's and Carnap's 'content-measure' and, additivity included, to their 'measure of information'. There is thus no basis for any separation of 'semantic information theory' from the general theory of information as defined in the Appendix.

MEANING

The foregoing recapitulation of the scope and the concepts of information theory provides a framework on which to hang our discussion of the concept of meaning. At the outset we must note that it is not only statements which may be said to have meaning. We speak also of the 'meaning' of other expressions such as questions, commands and even exclamations. In seeking to define an equivalent of the term in the language of information theory, we must be careful not to imply too narrow a definition.

I do not mean that we must find an omnibus equivalent which can be substituted directly for all uses of 'meaning' in everyday speech; but it does seem reasonable for the reader to demand, and the information-theorist to accept, the principle that, in the early stages particularly, the technical equivalent of a common term should conform as far as possible with common usage. The technician's effort to sharpen the concept should at least in principle allow the technical equivalent to be substituted for the term, without violation of basic sense or grammar, in as many contexts as possible.

Let us now picture a communication process in which you send a message (M) to me. For example, M might be 'Someone is waiting for you outside'. Now we may assume that by sending M to me you intend to produce some effect on me. If you had sent a message in gibberish or in a language unknown to me, you might have intended only to distract and puzzle me; but since the message M is in English, we will take it that you intend me to understand it and to appreciate its meaning. What kind of effect is this? Obviously it need not be an immediate change in my observable pattern of behaviour. What you are concerned with is my 'total state of readiness': in objective terms, the set or matrix of conditional probabilities of different possible patterns of behaviour in relevant circumstances. For example, when I leave the room you want me to behave as if I expected to find someone outside, and so forth. It is, then, the conditional-probability matrix or 'C.P.M.' which you want to affect in a particular way, by my 'understanding the meaning' of your message. If the C.P.M. is already in the desired state — if for example I know already that someone is waiting for me — then your object has already been achieved. Your object, then, is not necessarily to bring about a change in the C.P.M., but to establish a certain state of (part of) the C.P.M. for activity, internal (e.g. perceptual) or external (e.g. motor activity).

What then of the meaning of your message? We must clearly distinguish between (*a*) the meaning intended by the sender, (*b*) the meaning understood by the receiver, and (*c*) the conventional meaning. But if we take (*b*), for example, can we define the received meaning as simply the change that takes place in B's behaviour? Attempts have been made to define the meaning of a message simply as the behaviour-pattern it produces in the receiver; but this I think will not do. To begin with, we would not say that a message has no meaning if the receiver already knows what it is saying. A message does not lose its *meaning* through being repeated. And then purely on linguistic grounds one could scarcely regard the behaviour resulting from receipt of a message as synonymous with its received meaning. Any number of sentences in which 'meaning' is normally used would become grammatical nonsense, if this 'definition' were substituted.

On the other hand, the received meaning is certainly closely tied up with the behavioural consequences, if we include internal as well as external activity under 'behaviour'. We may reasonably say that the consequent internal and external behaviour-pattern in principle shows or demonstrates the received meaning.

Can we then define the received meaning as the change in the C.P.M. for internal and external activity? Again our objection would apply, that a repeated message may produce no significant change. Can we identify the meaning with the state of the C.P.M. rather than the change? Again the linguistic objections are I think conclusive. The meaning of a message is not identical with the state it produces. It is *identified by* the state it produces. This represents some progress. A message read for a second time produces — or should produce — substantially the same state of the relevant C.P.M. Its meaning is the same. What technically precise phrase can we substitute then for 'meaning' here?

I suggest that the received meaning of the message be defined, not as the resulting state of the C.P.M. but as *the selective function of the message on an ensemble of possible states of the C.P.M.* 'Selective function' here implies of course a relationship, not a happening.

Tentatively we take as our basic definition of 'meaning', then, the selective function on a specified set or ensemble, or for short 'selective function'. This leaves room for as many subdivisions of the concept as there are different definable ensembles; but I have not yet come across any instances in which one cannot consistently replace 'meaning' by 'selective function' or 'selective operation', leaving the sense unaltered, and giving often considerable illumination.

Corresponding to our distinctions between intended, received, and conventional meaning, we now have distinctions between (*a*) the selective function intended by the originator; (*b*) the selective function actually exercised; (*c*) the selective function on the ensemble of states of a conventional symbolic representational system.

In what follows we shall not always recapitulate these, but the necessary modifications to the argument to make it apply in cases (*a*), (*b*), or (*c*) will be obvious.

SOME TEST CASES

Let us take a few examples. To begin with, let us consider the term 'meaningless'. 'This message or word is meaningless', on our definition, becomes 'This message or word lacks a selective function...it has no selective relationship to....' To what? Immediately our definition suggests that the statement '*X* is meaningless' is incomplete. This we should expect, for a sentence may easily be meaningful to one man and gibberish to another. Meaninglessness is a relative concept, and a precise definition of meaning would be useless unless it automatically reminded us of this.

Now it is possible for something to lack a selective function for two reasons: (*a*) one or more of its component terms may be undefined — may have no selective function — so that the total selective operation is undefined; (*b*) two or more of the component selective functions may be incompatible, so that the total selective operation cannot be completed.

Correspondingly, we find two kinds of meaningless sentence. 'The gups are plee' is meaningless to most of us for the first reason. 'The water is isosceles' is meaningless for the second. On the other hand, 'This stochastic process is stationary' is probably meaningless to most of our fellow-mortals for the first reason; and 'The radiation from a horn-fed cheese' (actual title of a paper on Microwaves!) perhaps equally meaningless for the second.

Consider next the notion of 'synonymy'. One objection to any attempt to define meaning is that 'Two concepts may have the same meaning on one definition of the term, but different meanings on another'. For example, does 'an equilateral plane figure with four right-angled corners' have the same meaning as 'a square'? Our answer is quite clear. If we translate 'meaning' by 'selective function' we see at once that identity of selective function (synonymy) is going to depend on the particular ensemble on which we propose to test the selective function. The fact that various proposed 'definitions' of meaning have given different answers from common sense may merely be evidence that they were not sufficiently fundamental. If attempts are made to define a relation in terms of only one of its terminals, we must expect apparent paradoxes to result. Thus 'an equilateral plane figure with four right-angled corners' has the same selective function as 'a square' on the ensemble of plane geometric figures. It may have quite a different selective function on the ensemble of my states of imaginative activity.

What then of a message which states something I know already or a message which is repeated? As long as we define the meaning as the selective function rather than the effect there is no paradox in the fact that the effect on second hearing may be negligible. The selective operator which formally represents the meaning of a message is usually (in mathematical jargon) '*idempotent*': the immediate repetition of the selective operation should yield an unchanged result. Admittedly the fact that it has been repeated may itself have meaning — may have a selective function of its own. This however is quite distinct from the meaning of the message itself which is unchanged.

Here we begin to renew contact with information theory. We are accustomed to saying that a mere repetition of the same message (in the absence of noise) has no selective-information-content for the receiver, because the ensemble on which it operates the second time has only one member with non-zero probability. Selective-information-content in fact measures the size of the change brought about by a given selective operation. A second hearing of our message causes no change, and so has no selective-information-content; but it has the same selective function and so on our definition the same meaning as before. If, on the other hand, it did not exercise the appropriate selective function on first hearing, we say it was misunderstood. Its selective function, and hence its received meaning, on second hearing may then be different.

It is of course a psychological fact that if the same phrase or sentence is repeated sufficiently often it temporarily loses its meaning. Here is a further test of our definition, and again it not only survives, but shows the phenomenon itself in a fresh light. Repetition robs a sentence of meaning-to-the-subject — of 'selective function on the ensemble of states of the subject's C.P.M.', we would say. This not only makes sense, but suggests various experimental questions as to the processes by which constant repetition of symbolic stimuli leads temporarily to their 'uncoupling' from the selective system governing the subject's C.P.M.

So we might go on. The meaning (intended, received, conventional) of a command, a question, or an exclamation, for example, can likewise be defined as their selective function on a specified ensemble of responses. The detailed discussion of questions, commands, and other non-descriptive messages would have taken us too far, but the outlines of their treatment from the present standpoint will probably be clear enough. For the moment it is sufficient to note that our technical definition of meaning appears to be equally applicable in all such cases. Differences there are in plenty, but they are differences in the ensemble on which selective function is exercised, rather than differences in the basic concept of meaning in each case.

One remaining use of 'meaning' is in a rather different category. We sometimes speak of the meaning of objects or events which are not messages. An overcast sky 'means' that rain is imminent; or a mud-pie on the front doorstep 'means' that the children have been playing there.

Here the object is a sign of what it 'means', but not a symbol. It thus does not have an intended or a conventional selective function; but the meaning which we attribute to it can still be defined as its selective function on the ensemble of states of our C.P.M. The concept of meaning once again admits of one and the same definition.

THE RELEVANT ENSEMBLES

At this point — if not before — an objection may well be raised. Not everything which alters the total C.P.M. for activity is a message; nor would it necessarily be described as meaningful. Thus our definition might seem to be too broad.

In one sense it certainly is. We have seen already that in any particular case we must fill it out by specifying whether the selective function is intended, actual, or conventional, and saying for what ensemble it is defined. Our purpose has been to discover, if we can, a satisfactory basic concept from which the various common senses of 'meaning' can be derived by making these various distinctions. By extracting the common factor of 'selective function' (i.e. selective relationship to an ensemble specified or implied) we have, I hope, found the first term in a 'family tree' of sub-definitions which we must expect to ramify as widely as the range of relevant ensembles.

On the other hand, a definition of meaning must not be mistaken for a sufficient criterion of meaningfulness. Our object is to provide a technical equivalent for the term 'meaning' where it is in fact used, not to legislate as to where it should be used. The latter is largely an empirical task — to discover, if we can, the range of relevant ensembles presupposed in our basic definition of meaning. Here we may note only a few pointers.

First, what distinguishes the perception of a meaningful object or event from that of a meaningless one? Essentially, the first leads or could lead to a further inference. To say 'X means Y' is to imply that a further representation, Y, is logically justified, given X. Even to say 'X is meaningful' is to imply that some further representational activity is logically justified by X, whether or not the speaker is able to carry it out.

Thus the range of ensembles to which a meaningful object or event has a selective relationship by virtue of its meaning is restricted to those of representational states. In the human organism, for example, we may presume that there are certain internal states of the information flow system which constitute implicit representations of the subject's world of activity, both conceptual and physical.

To ask in detail what characterizes representational states of the information flow system would take us too far, and I have discussed the question elsewhere.[15] But we may draw one more basic dividing line. A typical pattern of activity — say walking out of the room expecting to find a friend outside the door — is directed to the achievement of a hierarchy of 'goals': to maintain balance, to avoid the corner of the table, to find the door handle, and so forth. If the table, for example, is moved, the corresponding 'goal-setting' alters if I become aware that it has moved. The hierarchy of goal-settings represents, in a definite sense, what I know or believe concerning my world of activity. Our suggestion is, briefly, that the internal representational activity of the human organism takes the form of the selection of goal-settings — including the conditional probabilities of their alteration. The ensembles presupposed in our definition of meaning are ensembles of goal-settings in the above sense.

What then of 'conventional meaning', as given for example in dictionaries? What an entry in a dictionary does is to replace an unfamiliar selective operator by an equivalent whose selective function for the user is presumed to be established. The ensemble concerned is in the first instance that of established selective operators; but the term 'established' presupposes a 'standard user' whose ensemble of representational states is ultimately in question.

This discussion applies equally to natural and to artificial languages. The only difference is that whereas natural sentences may modify the C.P.M. (state of readiness) for other than symbolic responses, sentences in an artificial language affect only the C.P.M. for perception and manipulation of the symbols themselves.

MECHANICAL TRANSLATION

Our present line of thought has a bearing on the vexed question of mechanical translation. When as children we learn to translate from one language to another we may begin by trying to substitute one word directly for another with the help of a dictionary. As we progress, we gradually pass over to a quite different kind of procedure. We try to discover what the original author *wants to convey* in the new language. In short, we pass over from thinking solely in terms of the *symbols* to thinking in terms of the *dispositions intended to be evoked* by the symbols. This is what distinguishes insightful translation from what some would prefer to call mere transcription.

A corresponding distinction exists between two different approaches which are covered by the name of mechanical translation. The first, at present almost universal, produces a translation by a correlation of syntactic structure in the two languages. No understanding is needed, in principle, of the dispositions intended to be evoked by the material to be translated. For this reason I would suggest that even Professor Yngve's ingenious 'transition language'[41] would perhaps be better termed a 'transition code', since its function is not to select dispositions but rather symbols.

The second approach would be to make, as an intermediate step, a representation of the *dispositions* intended to be evoked by the material to be translated. A translation could then be achieved by producing, as the output, expressions in the other language which evoked the same dispositions. I know of no practical work being carried out on these lines, and I suspect that it may have to wait for our understanding of information-processing in the human organism; but the product of such a translating device would, I think, be much closer to what we normally desire of a human translator. The difference would be shown most easily in the kinds of fault to which each translation would be liable. A translation on the first principle should quite faithfully reflect the syntactic structure of the original, but could easily fail seriously to convey the meaning. A translation on the second principle might allow only a loose inference to the syntactic structure of the original, but should on the whole faithfully reproduce its meaning.

'MEANING' IN THE FORMALISM OF INFORMATION THEORY

We may now seek to connect this approach with the author's earlier representation of meaning in the formalism of information theory. The state of a representational system can be described by enumerating the states of each of its independent degrees of freedom. If there are l of these, each may be associated with one dimension of an l-dimensional 'information-space', so that any given state is represented by a point or region of this space.

A particular message may now be pictured as selecting a particular region, which may be identified by the vector (or distribution of vectors) linking it to the origin. The meaning of the message is then represented by the orientation of this vector, relative to the vector basis. Where the meaning is imprecise, the selective operation is imprecise, and the orientation of the vector correspondingly distributed statistically.

Some further details of this representation have been discussed in Chapter 6. For the moment we note only that the orientation of the vector specifies and corresponds one-to-one with the selective function of the message. The two approaches thus unite in an illuminating way, since the term 'selective function', although the best I can suggest at the moment, is not ideally explicit; and the orientation of a selective 'arrow' provides a useful thought-model of what is intended by the term.

Conclusions

(1) It appears from our investigation that the theory of information has a natural, precise, and objectively definable place for the concept of meaning.

(2) The meaning of a message may be defined as its selective function on a specified ensemble.

(3) The selective-information-content of the message measures logarithmically the size of the change brought about by its selective operation on the same ensemble.

(4) The relevant ensemble comprises different possible states of a representational system. In the human organism these are states of the conditional-probability matrix (C.P.M.)

governing goal-setting activity. Where the human C.P.M. is in question, the relevant probabilities cannot of course be estimated objectively (nor, probably, subjectively). This does not, however, prevent the concept from being objectively defined; nor does it preclude the possibility that these probabilities are determined by an objectively definable physical state of the organism.

(5) The basic concept of meaning as selective function subdivides according to the ensembles for which the function is defined. The distinctions between intended meaning, received meaning, and conventional meaning are automatically preserved.

(6) It may be too much to expect that every idiomatic usage of 'meaning' will be adequately translated by 'selective function', but the concept seems to apply equally readily in relation to questions, commands, and other non-propositional utterances, and to non-symbolic objects possessing significance.

(7) Since meaning, as thus defined, has as fine gradations as the gradations of human C.P.M.'s, the ideal of an unambiguous universal language would seem to be unrealizable. The most hopeful ideal approximation would be a language the primitive individuals of which represented the independent degrees of freedom of the human C.P.M. which are common to all normal humans. It may well prove the best, if not the most practicable solution to the problems of context and the like in mechanical translation to use an ideal language based on this principle as an intermediary between the original and final languages. Unfortunately the completion of a truly basic language on these lines waits on our understanding of the human C.P.M.

CHAPTER 8

The Informational Analysis of Questions and Commands*

INTRODUCTION

It is not, I think, without significance that some recent symposia on information theory contain relatively few papers on the theory of information; but the significance is not, as might be supposed, that the theoretical concepts are now so far worked out that only their applications remain to be discussed. In fact the contrary would be nearer the truth: that most of us who began with an interest in the theoretical concept of information have become so increasingly and profitably absorbed in practical problems of information-processing, in animals or machines, that the general analysis of informational exchange has been largely by-passed, and for the majority of the new generation now leaving college information theory still means little more than Shannon's measure of unexpectedness and its various applications. Otherwise excellent leading textbooks unashamedly proclaim a divorce between what they call 'information theory' and semantics, which topic is discussed, if at all, in the woolliest terms, and generally relegated to the philosopher.

As this can hardly be regarded as an ideal state of affairs in

* From *Proceedings of 4th London Symposium on Information Theory*, 1960 (E. C. Cherry, ed.), Butterworths, pp. 469–76.

such a young subject, we may well ask why so little progress has been made on the semantic side. Apart from the absence of workers, I suspect the reason to lie in our failure to study the communicative process within a wide enough context: to follow the flow of information far enough back, and forward, from the communication channel. We are all familiar with diagrams showing the human sender and receiver as 'black box' terminals linked by a chain of noisy channels. My suggestion is that semantic questions find their natural place in information theory when (but only when) we widen our diagrams to take account of the nature of these terminals as *goal-directed* self-adaptive systems.

Our particular object will be to suggest how questions and commands can be analysed in informational terms similar to those outlined in earlier chapters for the analysis of indicative sentences. In the first part we shall sketch the informational requirements of organisms in the situation in which questions and commands are exchanged between them. Thus fortified, we shall try to discern some lines along which at least semi-quantitative analysis may fruitfully be pressed.

THE IMPACT OF INFORMATION ON THE ORGANISM

An organism can be regarded for our purpose as a system with a certain repertoire of basic acts (both internal and external) that in various combinations and sequences make up its behaviour. In order that its behaviour should be adaptive to its environment,* the selective process by which basic acts are concatenated requires to be *organized* according to the current state of the environment in relation to the organism. There are various ways of picturing this need. In its most basic terms, we may regard what is required as equivalent to a vast constantly changing matrix of *conditional probabilities* (the C.P.M.), determining the relative probabilities of various patterns (and patterns of patterns) of behaviour in all possible circumstances. More economically, we can think of it as the setting-up of a hierarchic structure of organizing 'sub-routines' to determine these conditional probabilities, [17,19] interlocked in such a way as to represent implicitly the structure of the environment (the world of activity) with which the organism must interact. For many purposes we may reduce it to the filling-out of a world-map, ready to be consulted according to current needs and goals.

* 'Environment' here means the total world of activity of the organism, and not only its immediate physical milieu.

Whatever our thought-model, it is clear that unless the organism happens to be organized exactly to match the current state of affairs, *work* must be done to bring it up to date: work not only in a physical, but in a *logical* sense. This 'logical work' consists in the adjusting and moulding of the conditional-probability structure of the organizing system: the formation, strengthening or dissolution of functional linkages between various basic acts or basic sequences of acts. The total configuration of these linkages embodies what we may call the total 'state of readiness' of the organism. Some of them will of course have purely vegetative functions that do not concern us. What does interest us is the total configuration that keeps the organism matched to its field of purposive activity, and so implicitly represents (whether correctly or not) the features of that field. For brevity, let us call this the *orienting* system, and the corresponding total state of readiness the *orientation* of the organism.

Information can now be defined as that which does logical work on the organism's orientation (whether correctly or not, and whether by adding to, replacing or confirming the functional linkages of the orienting system). Thus we leave open the question whether the information is true or false, fresh, corrective or confirmatory, and so on.

The *amount of information* received by an organism can then be measured (in various ways) by measuring if we can (in various ways) the logical (organizing) work that it does for the organism. I have discussed elsewhere some of the different measures that suggest themselves for different purposes, and we shall return briefly to the question later. Meanwhile it is sufficient to note that they are necessarily *relative* measures, since they measure the impact of information on the given receiver. 'Amount of information' measures not a 'stuff' but a relation.* The *meaning* of an indicative item of information to the organism may now be defined as its selective function on the range of the organism's possible states of orientation, or, for short, its *organizing function* for the organism. It will be noted that this too is a relation. (It must be clearly distinguished from the *organizing work done* on the organism, which is *the result of the exercise* of this organizing function. Much confusion is caused by attempts to identify meaning with the change produced in the receiver.)

PERCEPTION AND COMMUNICATION

A solitary organism keeps its orienting system up to date in response to physical *signs* of the state of the environment, received by its sense organs. This adaptive up-dating of the state of orientation we call *perception*. We can regard *communication* as an extension of this process whereby some of the organizing work in one organism is attempted by *another*

---

* This does not of course make the concept any less objective in principle, since one can always postulate a 'standard receiver', and this is in effect what is done in communication theory; but it does prevent the magnitude associated with it from having a unique value. The same item can have quite different information-contents for different receivers.

organism. Normally this means that the receiving organism is induced to adapt itself in response to physical signs that are perceived as *symbols* — as calling for orienting (or other) activity over and above that which constitutes their perception as physical events.*

The logical starting point for a semantic theory of communication would therefore seem to be the analysis of the organizing functions that are 'extensible' in this way from one organism to another. There is a sense in which for this purpose the analysis of questions is logically prior to that of indicative sentences; for the meaning of an indicative sentence is often ambiguous until we know the *question* to which it is an answer, and/or the assertion which it *excludes*. For example, the sentence S: 'I sleep in room 10' may be an answer to the question (*a*) 'Where do you sleep?' or (*b*) 'Do you sleep in room 10 or room 12?' or (*c*) 'Who sleeps in room 10?' or (*d*) 'What do you use room 10 for?' and so on. Typical assertions excluded by S are then respectively (*a*) 'I sleep elsewhere...' (*b*) 'I sleep in room 12' (*c*) 'Someone else sleeps in room 10' (*d*) 'I use room 10 for other purposes'.†

Clearly, the selective function of S is quite different in these cases, either in its range (as between (*a*) and (*b*)) or in its dimensions (as between (*a*), (*c*) and (*d*)). No analysis of its semantic information-content can claim to be adequate unless it brings out differences of this sort, as well as doing justice to logical structure.

Questions

What then in these terms constitutes a *question*? The *object* of a question is normally to evoke communicative activity of the sort we have been discussing; but this by itself would be far from a definitive notion. Again the *linguistic form* of a

* The training process by which symbols come to be accepted as such need not here concern us.

† For a useful discussion of this point see M. and A. Prior: 'Erotetic Logic' (ref. 28). It should be noted that in spoken, as opposed to written, speech the ambiguity is normally resolved by appropriate use of stress and intonation.

question is often characteristic, but not always. *Intonation* may sometimes be the key discriminant, as in a phrase like 'going home?' which could equally well be the *answer* to a question. What, however, are we to say of the sentence 'I take it that you are going home'? It would normally make sense to treat this as a question requiring the same answer as 'Are you going home?'; yet it is in form (and could be in intonation) a plain indicative statement.

But indicative of what? Here I think we come to the heart of the matter. What is indicated here is the *state of readiness* of the originator, in relation to the receiver; and this points to a characteristic of all questions. A question is basically a purported *indication of inadequacy* in its originator's state of readiness, calculated to elicit some organizing work to remedy the inadequacy. It is as if the questioner uncovered and held out the incomplete part of his organizing system to the receiver for his attention.

The fact that this normally works reveals an interesting presupposition behind the whole procedure. We may well ask why the receiver should be expected to pay any responsive attention of this sort to the exposed organizing system; and the answer is clear. Questions work only because human beings are *motivated* to adjust one another's states of readiness. Whether thanks to nature or nurture, a human being finds an organizing system 'exposed' in this deliberate way by another a natural target for adaptive activity, much as a mother bird is moved to regard a gaping beak in the nest. Doubtless were it not so the human race would hardly have survived!

The moral would seem to be that what makes an utterance a question cannot always be pinned down either to a peculiarity of its logical form (since an inadequacy of orientation can be indicated in many ways, some of them wordless) nor to the fact that it has elicited information (since people are liable spontaneously to try to adjust one another's orientation).

Our problem in fact has some affinity with that of determining whether a given action was 'goal-directed' towards a certain end-point. Neither the form nor the effect of the action are infallible criteria alone. Instead, we adopt a 'variational' approach[15] and look for evidence (usually structural) that if the 'goal' had been slightly displaced, or the starting point slightly different, the form of action would have been correspondingly modified in a manner calculated to reach the same end-point.

Similarly we can determine some utterances to be a question only, in the end, by inquiring how the behaviour of the originator would have been modified in varying circumstances: in other words, by examining the total information-flow-map within which the utterance originated.

For many purposes, however, this is too stringent a test. An examiner, for example, may frame a question to which he already knows the answer. His object is to gain, not the information represented by the answer, but information as to whether the condidate knows the answer. Yet the candidate would be ill-advised to ignore the utterance on the ground that the examiner was not really asking a question. Here the form, in its context, is decisive. A properly framed examination question depicts an inadequacy in the orientation of an imaginary questioner, and the candidate is expected to show his prowess by an answer calculated to remedy the inadequacy in a typical originator.* We may perhaps take as our tentative definition of a question, then, a combination of an *indication* and an *invitation*: or, if we like, a two-fold indication, (*a*) of inadequacy in orientation, and (*b*) of desire to have it remedied by the receiver.

THE MEANING OF A QUESTION

The purpose of an indicative statement is to bring up to date some aspect of the receiver's state of readiness. Conversely, the main ostensible purpose of a question is to bring

---

* The question here is merely being 'mentioned' by the examiner, and not 'used', as it would be by a typical originator.

about, as it were by remote control, an updating of the questioner's *own* state of readiness. He wants the receiver to do some organizing work on him. The primary meaning of a question, then, which we might call its *interrogative meaning*, can be defined, like the meaning of an indicative sentence, as its selective function; but it selects from the range of possible orienting operations *on the questioner himself.* Its job is to identify the organizing work that needs to be done on the originator's switchboard, so to say. The meaning of the answer will in turn be its selective function — a more detailed one — on the range of the questioner's states of orientation. Its job is to set the switches.

On the other hand, as we have seen, a question also plays an indicative role, by simply showing the receiver the inadequacy of the questioner's state of readiness, together with his desire to have it remedied. It is therefore worth while to distinguish the *indicative meaning* of a question as (for short) its orienting function for the receiver. It is obviously quite possible for a question to be interrogatively meaningful while indicatively meaningless, and vice versa. Interrogatively, a question is meaningless when it *calls for* no orienting work on the *originator*; indicatively, it is meaningless when it *performs* none on the *receiver.*

Thus to ask 'where does the flame go when the gas is turned off?' is interrogatively meaningless as it stands, because if we assume that 'flame' means 'gas being burned', the two halves of the question call for mutually incompatible selective functions. When there is no gas, there is no flame to go anywhere. But it is not indicatively meaningless, for its utterance does orient the receiver with respect to the questioner's muddled organizing system.

REQUESTS AND COMMANDS

We have pictured the asking of a question as offering the receiver access to some of the originator's controls. Conversely, we may now think of the uttering of a request or command as *seeking* or *claiming* access to some of the receiver's controls. It is perhaps hardly necessary in detail to go over all the corresponding ground. The controls in question are now those that determine goal-setting and action, rather than map-making and orientation. The relationship is potentially one of much greater subordination than that of a questioner to his respondent, since a request or command (if accepted) supplants the process of calculation-in-view-of-goals by which the action would normally be determined, and on which the response to a question would bear.

Once again, as those with memories of nursery (or Army) language know well, we would be unwise to try to characterize a command by its logical form, though of course the 'imperative' if used is distinctive. 'Johnny, I want you to stop banging on the floor'; or (in the United States) 'Do you want to pass me the salt?' are cautionary samples of well-understood requests or commands to which the response required is not 'Oh' or 'Yes', respectively, but *action*.

A request or command then, as a communicative act, is basically an indication that action on the part of the receiver is necessary to remove disequilibrium in the originator: in other words, that the receiver is an intermediate *target* within the goal-system of the originator — that one of the originator's information-flow loops for goal-direction passes through him, so that he is potentially under feedback. Once again, the 'variational' question — what would happen in the originator's organizing system *if* the receiver did not act appropriately? — is the reliably diagnostic one, rather than analysis of form or effect in isolation.

Clearly we must again distinguish two semantic functions for a request or command. As its primary purpose is to select a goal-setting in the receiver, we may define its *imperative meaning* as its selective function on the range of the receiver's goal-settings. Inevitably, however, it also serves to indicate the goal-settings of the originator, so that its *indicative meaning* may be distinguished for short as its orienting function relative to the originator's goal-settings.

The usual distinctions between meaning-to-originator, meaning-to-receiver, and conventional meaning, can be made in obvious ways in each case. They are of course essential if ambiguity is to be avoided.

Quantitative Aspects

There is now no difficulty in principle in defining a measure of *selective information-content* for questions and commands, as for indicative sentences. In each case we may define it as the equivalent number of independent binary selective operations specified by the selective function in question.

For many purposes, however, we may be interested in the form as well as the magnitude of the selective operation; and here, as with indicative sentences, the structure of the organizing system would seem to offer a natural basis for quantification. I have argued elsewhere[19] for a model organized hierarchically, in which 'organizing sub-routines' at a given level are themselves organized by sub-routines at a deeper* level representing more abstract concepts.

If a model of this sort is correct, then an important quantitative parameter of a question will be the *order-number* of the level of organization at which it betokens an inadequacy. To take a simple example, a question of the form 'Is *A*, *B*?' is of a lower order than one of the form 'Are *all A*, *B*?'. 'Does the road next bend to left or right?' is of lower order than 'Is there any regularity in the sequence of bends?'. Similarly the command 'Turn left' is of lower order than the command 'Turn alternately left and right'. The second selects an *organizer of the organizers* dealt with by the first.

A second parameter of great importance will be the logical dimensionality (*logon-content*) of the question or command, defined as the number of independent 'degrees of freedom' of the organizing operation concerned. Thus 'What is the temperature?' has an (interrogative) logon-content of 1. (Indicatively it has of course as many as required for identification of the originator's state of inadequacy.) 'How has the temperature varied during the day?' has as many logons as there are independent ordinates on the graph required, and so on.

---

* 'Deeper' and 'higher', oddly enough, seem to be interchangeable as indices of greater abstractness.

With non-numerical questions the actual estimation of logon-content waits, of course, on our knowledge of the human organizing hierarchy; but the concept may have its qualitative uses even now. For example, we can recognize the importance of *matching* the logon-content of an answer to that of a question. We all know that feeling of impatience with an answer that swamps us with data in unnecessary detail, or of frustration with one that leaves us short of some key item. What I am suggesting is not that numerical measures as such would be easy or even useful in such a case, but rather that a quantitative theory of what is going on might help to articulate our intuitions and sharpen our recommendations of a remedy in more complex cases. This, after all, is perhaps the main service to be rendered by any semantic theory of communication.

It would be of obvious practical importance, for example, to ascertain whether George Miller's[25] 'Magic number 7' represents a maximum logon-content for any useful unit-question (or answer, or command).

CONCLUSIONS

The main argument of this paper has been that the semantic informational analysis of questions and commands, as of indicative sentences, could be most naturally and least ambiguously carried out by analysis of their 'organizing function' with respect to the information-systems engaged. This requires a stronger link than exists at present between semantics and the study of behavioural organization; and it is not unlikely that the benefits could be mutual, for the theorist of organization might well gain significant clues in return; for example, from the logical structure of thesauri.

It is of course easier to make such suggestions than to carry them out, and I have done no more than to indicate a few possibilities. We have seen how measures of selective information-content, and concepts of meaning, can readily be defined on this basis for questions and commands; and we have

singled out the order-number (can we call it simply the
'order'?), and the logical dimensionality or 'logon-content',
as two measures likely to be important. We have also noted
the importance of distinguishing between measures of 'indicative' function and those of interrogative and imperative
function, and between intended, received and conventional
meanings and information-contents.

But I am painfully aware that the bulk of what needs to be
done is little reduced by all this. If it succeeds only in stirring
up fruitful discussion in a neglected area it will have served its
purpose.

CHAPTER 9

Communication and Meaning — a Functional Approach[*]

FOREWORD

The Wenner-Gren Symposium on Cross-Cultural Understanding (1962) brought together a group that included anthropologists, biologists, linguists, and philosophers. My brief was to outline the scope of the theory of information in its most general sense, and to consider what light it might throw on the problem of cross-cultural communication. A large section dealing with information-measurement has here been omitted, but the remainder has been reproduced unabbreviated despite some overlap with earlier chapters.

INTRODUCTION

My purpose in this paper is to outline an approach to human behaviour from the standpoint of communication science, which may serve as a link between the study of individual man and that of social groups. Since both the human organism and the human group are systems that 'run on information', it may be of some interest to ask what informational mechanisms may embody the processes that anthropologists study.

Man as a mechanism is (as we have seen in earlier papers) a teleological or goal-directed system. In a general sense, we

* From *Cross-Cultural Understanding*, edited by F. S. C. Northrop and Helen Livingston, New York, Harper and Row, 1964, pp. 162–79. Copyright © 1964 by Wenner-Gren Foundation for Anthropological Research, Incorporated.

can say that information as to the current state of his environment (including results of his own activity) contributes to the ongoing selective process by which his behaviour is organized.[19,29] The numerous goals of the human system form a partially-ordered hierarchy, such that many goal-settings are under the control of 'superior' sub-systems. The setting of such goals, in other words, constitutes a *means* to a (temporarily or permanently) dominant end. Thus for a solitary man the acquisition of a tool, or the turning of a control knob, may be a sub-goal prescribed by superior goal-directed calculations. Since the rank-ordering of sub-goals generally depends on current information as to the state of the field of action, we need a term which covers both the current goal-settings and the 'matrix of conditional probabilities' which determines what change *would* take place *if* such and such information were received. Let us refer to this as the 'goal-complex' of the system.

When the environment includes other members of the same (or sufficiently similar) species, a new kind of possibility emerges. In addition to the ordinary methods of interaction, the individual now has the possibility of influencing his environment by way of another individual, by inducing changes in that individual's goal-complex. This latter is the process we call communication. Clearly, it introduces the further possibility of back-reaction from the second individual to the first, directed towards alteration in *his* goal-complex. Where this is the case (as normally in dialogue) it may become logically impossible to dissociate the two goal-complexes. The individuals have acquired a relationship in which their individualities have partly merged. They constitute for certain purposes a single goal-directed system. For these purposes, it becomes meaningful to refer to them as a social unit.

THE CONCEPT OF INFORMATION

Human beings modify one another's goal-complexes in a variety of ways. We make indicative statements, ask questions, issue requests and commands. To summarise discussions presented elsewhere (Chapters 7 and 8), it seems possible to distinguish fairly clearly between the mechanical aspects of such processes, by looking at their different effects on the goal-complexes involved.

Remembering that the goal-complex embodies implicitly a representation of 'what is believed to be the case', as well as the hierarchy of goals being pursued, we may distinguish between two kinds of change which can be effected by an utterance: between two kinds of 'target' which an individual's goal-complex presents to his interlocutor. The first target is the current 'map', or representation of the state of affairs, implicit in his goal-complex. The second is the current content and rank-order of the goal-hierarchy.

An *indicative* utterance is goal-directed towards the completion or alteration of the 'map' implicit in the *recipient's* goal-complex — i.e. it is uttered as a means of alerting his system to the situation indicated by the utterance; and any sign that it did not have the required effect on the recipient's 'map' would normally evoke further corrective or adaptive action by the originator.

An *interrogative* utterance, on the other hand, is goal-directed towards the 'up-dating' of the *originator's own* 'map'. The recipient becomes a link in the forward path of an action-under-feedback, whose goal is the filling-up of an inadequacy in the originator's state of readiness. Of course the utterance cannot help having an indicative aspect as well: it alerts the recipient to the inadequacy it reveals in the originator. That this is not normally its primary goal may be seen, however, by asking what would happen if the originator's inadequacy were remedied without the recipient's realising its nature and extent.

The way in which analogous functional distinctions may be drawn between other types of utterance will now be obvious, and need not here be laboured. Imperative utterances, for example, have as their primary target the goal-structure rather than the orienting 'map' of the recipient; and so forth.

I have mentioned these technicalities only because I think that a coherent account of semantics requires us to widen our view of the communicative process (so often discussed only in terms of source, channel and sink) to include the whole pattern of goal-directed activities within which it plays a part. In ordinary subjective terms, to have one's 'map' brought up to date is to receive 'information'. 'Information-about-X' is that which *determines the form* of one's state-of-readiness for X. In objective terms exactly parallel statements

108   *CHAPTER 9*

can be made about the human mechanism, by replacing 'one's' by 'its'. In short, to talk in terms of 'information', 'determination-of-form', 'map', 'goal', 'state-of-readiness', and the like, provides us with a common conceptual language in which it is relatively easy to make connections between correlated subjective and objective data that concern us. Up to a point, we can even frame definitions that can be used interchangeably at the two levels.

The concept of information that emerges in these terms is essentially *relative*. I have suggested elsewhere that we define 'information', in isolation, as 'that which determines form'. This definition has the advantage of applying equally well to what 'flows' along artificial communication lines and what 'passes' between human beings; but it still invites us to ask: 'the form of *what*?' Conceptually our picture is incomplete unless we specify what information is *about* — what it represents or betokens. In other words, the concept of information is inseparable from that of *meaning*.

THE CONCEPT OF MEANING

The purpose of communication being the modification of goal-complexes (in recipient and/or originator), it seems possible to define the *meaning* of a communication as its *selective function* on the range of possible states of the goal-complex concerned. We could perhaps abbreviate this to its '*orienting function*'.

Note first that this too is a *relative* concept, allowing essential distinctions to be drawn (in obvious ways) between (e.g.) meaning-to-originator and meaning-to-recipient, and between indicative, interrogative and imperative meanings.

We may note further the difference between this definition in terms of selective *function*, and attempts to define meaning as the *effect produced* in the recipient. The effect produced by a message may well *betoken* its meaning; but it would be absurdly restrictive to *equate* it with the meaning. It may be true that (e.g.) if meaning is vague and ill-defined, the effect produced is also vague and ill-defined. In that sense many terms that qualify 'meaning' can also qualify 'effect produced'; but the conceptual reduction of 'meaning' to 'effect' represents in fact a confusion between a *function* and the result of its *exercise*.*

* The point here is related to the distinction made in mathematics between the concept of a (mathematical) function and that of its numerical values — a distinction clarified only after much labour by d'Alembert and his successors.

At the risk of oversimplification, we might liken the meaning of a message to the 'opening power' of a key in relation to a given lock. To turn the key has the *effect* of opening the lock, but the opening (a change in the lock) merely *betokens* the opening power of the key, and cannot be equated with it. Opening power is a property of the *key* (in relation to that lock) which could in principle be established by inspection of lock and key, even if the key were never used.

Similar objections can clearly be made to the dictum that 'the meaning is the use'. Its intention to be 'operational' is laudable; but it fastens upon the wrong operation. In the case of our key, the operation required is to look inside the mechanism of the lock, and see what *would* happen *if* the key were used. In the case of a human recipient, the corresponding operation may well be impracticable for good social and surgical reasons; but this is no excuse for Procrustean distortion of the conceptual picture. Not even the most hardened operationalist pretends that all his 'operations' could be performed in practice: what matters is that they are possible in principle; and in principle (if our notions of the causal organisation of behaviour are at all valid) the orienting function of a message (*qua* potential input) could be determined just as readily by advance inspection of the brain, as the opening power of a key by advance inspection of the lock.

It may be only fair to point out that what the slogan 'meaning is use' was meant to reject is equally strongly excluded by our present definition — namely, the idea that meaning could be defined solely in terms of the form of the message. While for many purposes we may discuss the meaning of utterances safely enough in terms of their orienting function for a 'standard recipient', it would be philosophical folly to conclude from this that meaning was an absolute property of an utterance, definable without reference to any recipient. This would be like arguing that the 'opening power' of a master key was an absolute property of its profile, definable without reference to any lock.

Simply by asking what gives any physical event-sequence the status of a communication, we can detect the reference to specific goal-complexes implicit in even the most artificial 'languages' of the logician. Thus, for example, it is not the rules that give meaning to the moves in a game of chess. What introduces the element of meaning is surely the *agreement of players* to abide by those rules: that is, to adopt a standard pair of (sub-) goal-complexes. The moves can be said to have their chess meaning (selective function) only in relation to those goal-complexes. The movement of a black pawn may mean to the 'white' player a threat, to the 'black' player a relief, and to an ignorant onlooker the displacement of a piece of carved wood. Each reveals his goal-complex (artificial or natural) by the meaning he assigns. In each case, at the mechanical level, we may expect corresponding differences between the respective 'states of readiness' upon which it impinges, to account for the diverse effects of the same physical stimulus.

One final point of great importance should be noted. Our definition of meaning places no restriction on the *levels* of the goal-complex upon which selective function may be exercised. Since many sub-goals in the human system concern internal bodily states (e.g. visceral or hormonal) of which the agent himself may not be articulately conscious, it is impossible to regard the full meaning of an utterance to an individual as always coextensive with what he can (even in principle) *say* it means. To say what something means to one is to try to fabricate other verbal selective operators, with identical function; but if one's power of introspection is limited (as psychologists tell us it is) then this is only a crude and approximate performance at best. The selective function of an utterance for an individual may obviously be perfectly well-defined, although he can *say* nothing well-defined about it. It seems important to rid ourselves of the current heresy that only what can be expressed precisely in words has precise meaning. Once again, we may lack opportunity in *practice* to observe the selective functioning of an utterance on the mechanism embodying a human goal-complex; but simply to envisage it in principle should be enough to unsettle any dogmatic restriction of meaningfulness to what can be described in words.

Conversely, it is clear that from our present standpoint an utterance needs to be viewed as a physical whole if we are to make proper sense of its semantic function. Important though the phonemic aspects of the physical stimulus may be, its selective function for a given recipient has other determinants (such as intonation, rhythm, and context or background) which in some cases may completely dominate the operation on his goal-complex. Only our lack of a conventional notation for these other (equally potent) features of utterance can explain the extent to which they are ignored, in our legal and social conceptions of truth-telling and lying, for example.

Everybody knows at heart that for some purposes the phonemic reduction of an utterance can be as dangerously inept as a black-and-white photograph of a traffic light. If the investigation of other people's ideas is ever to have the status of an exact science, ways *must* be found to articulate and document all the salient features of the communicative process. There would seem to be no fundamental obstacle to our doing so eventually — or at least doing better than at present — along lines suggested by our present approach; but to say so is of course to sketch a programme rather than a solution.

FAILURE OF COMMUNICATION

The same analysis that enables us to handle the concept of meaning throws interesting light on the different ways in which the communicative process can *break down*. As 'failure of communication' must be one of the anthropologist's most common sources of frustration, it may be as well to sketch its formal features explicitly from our present viewpoint.

Failure may be partial or total. In every case, it means that the intended and actual selective functions differ significantly — i.e. sufficiently to transgress the originator's 'criterion of mismatch'.

Since the originator has the double task of envisaging the goal-complex (the 'lock') upon which he wants to operate, and of designing and emitting a stimulus (the 'key') with the required orienting function, he can fail if either the 'lock' or his 'key' is significantly different in fact from what he believes or intends it to be. At the worst, his effort can be 'meaningless'.

Total meaninglessness can be defined simply as 'absence of orienting function' (relative to a given recipient). Clearly, we must then distinguish between the meaninglessness of (*a*) *undefined* utterances (where no structure in the recipient's goal-complex has been pre-established to match the stimuli) and that of (*b*) *illegitimate* utterances (where the established selective functions of different components of an utterance are incompatible). Examples of each respectively might be (*a*) 'the jolks preed'; (*b*) 'the milk is isosceles'.

For the anthropologist, partial breakdown of communication (distortion of meaning) may present the more subtle problem. Clearly (in terms of our 'lock-and-key' image) such distortion of the intended orienting function can arise from ignorance of the 'lock', or faulty design and/or use of the 'key'. The problems of design and use will not be further elaborated. Ignorance of the 'lock', however, has two radically different aspects that merit discussion.

First (to drop the metaphor), the originator has to discover and understand the *goals and sub-goals* of the recipient. Apart from certain major goals common to all human beings, this may present difficulty enough. Yet by far the biggest problem arises at the second step — the elucidation of the principles on which these goals and sub-goals are hierarchically ordered to form the goal-complex.

I have suggested elsewhere [14,19] that the internal representation of the world of an organism may be thought of as a statistical model of the 'pattern of demand' made by the world upon the organism. By the 'pattern of demand' I mean not merely those features of the world (such as heat and cold) that bear upon and disturb the equilibrium of the inert organism, but all those that the active organism has to take into account when conducting goal-directed activity. The suggestion is that the organising system developed to match this pattern of demand (to do the necessary 'taking into account') can *itself* serve as the internal representation of the world.

It follows from this (if true) that the categories in terms of which the world is perceived and conceived of will depend on the various ways in which it has been found to thwart, facilitate and mould the pursuit of the organism's particular goals. Aspects of the world which call forth (or have received) no adaptive internal 'matching response' will simply fail to be perceived or conceived of.

The conceptual structure of the world so perceived will obviously be closely bound up with the structure of the organizing system. If, for example, a regular pattern appears in the sequence of demand, then the internal organizer that is evolved to 'match' it adaptively will constitute an internal symbol for that pattern. Wherever that pattern recurs, whether in the input, or in the internal traffic among the organisers themselves, it is likely to arouse this organiser. The concept which it represents will then be a constituent of the new situation as perceived.

Thus, in general, complex situations will tend to find themselves 'matched' (internally represented) by the best possible (hierarchic) combination of the basic organisers that previous experience of goal-pursuit has evolved in that individual. Conceptual innovation will not of course be impossible,[21,23] but in the absence of sufficient incentive and/or suitable training there are liable to be epistemological blind spots in conceptual areas to which no readily formed combination of organisers corresponds.*

Clearly, with a different pattern of past experience, or a different set of goal-priorities, it is possible for one human organism to have evolved a single complex organiser to represent a feature of the world almost (if not quite) beyond the conceptual grasp of another, whose organising system could cope with it only at the cost of major dismantling and rebuilding operations. Since the same is likely to be true in reverse, we have here a most potent and subtle source of failure of human communication. The point I would stress is that in these situations mere ostensive definition and exposure to common stimuli offers no remedy. The two individuals simply do not have the same perceptual experience when confronted with the same stimuli, so that ostensive naming could only breed further confusion. Any approach, to be

---

* Mathematical readers may be reminded of similar limitations to the usefulness of (e.g.) Fourier series as descriptions of waveforms. Although in theory any waveform can be described as the sum of sine waves, in practice the method becomes infinitely cumbersome for impulse-type functions. The language of frequency-analysis has a 'blind spot' for the concept of 'sudden change'.

fruitful, must start farther back, by probing the respective goal-hierarchies for the disparity of priorities which has made the conceptual framework of the world turn out so differently for each individual. The participants must not be surprised if beyond a certain point the process ceases to be academic and becomes (in today's jargon) 'existential'. For what we have been uncovering is one of the relations between human knowledge and human values. The goals pursued in life inevitably condition the terms in which life is perceived and understood. There can be a moral element in conceptual blindness.

What then of the implications for anthropology? Everyone knows the story of the medical missionaries in central Africa who discovered that to disclaim magical powers was equivalent to telling their tribespeople that they could not help them. But how effectively can we guard ourselves against the same kind of misunderstanding in reverse? Is it even possible in principle? To do so at all thoroughly, we should need to understand our own goal-complexes *from the outside* — and this smacks of 'pulling oneself up by one's own bootstraps'. Perhaps in the end the investigator's best hope is to enlist the aid of his subjects, in the endeavour to track down his own blind spots. He must realise, of course, that no process of this sort can do more than change the shape and location of these blind spots; but at least it should lead to the improvement of communication; and at best it may conceptually enrich one or both sides beyond their imagining.

Perhaps a fair illustration might be taken from the difficulty, even in his own civilisation, that faces the non-religious investigator of religious belief. However adequately he may feel that he has 'tied up' religious practice in his own categories, he cannot readily ignore the assurances of his subjects that his analysis, whose accuracy they may not dispute, is missing the point. If genuine religious commitment (as distinct from mere acceptance of credal affirmations) involves the uprooting of a 'self-centred' goal-structure and its gradual replacement by a new set of goal-priorities, then it is inevitable that, in pursuit of these, new categories and concepts become meaningful and relevant, even though (in the Christian religion for example) they do not necessarily render the old ones meaningless.

SOCIAL GROUPS AS INFORMATION SYSTEMS

In this concluding section we must glance at the overall significance of communicative processes within a social group. By way of introduction to the basic notions, imagine first two goal-seeking systems of equal power (two thermostatic air-conditioners will do) with incompatible goal-settings, and a common field of operation. In the ordinary way, each is bound to be driven by its feedback signal to run eventually 'flat out' in opposition to the other — one heating, the other cooling, so that the temperature lies somewhere between their two goal-settings.

How could this absurd and wasteful situation be resolved, or prevented from arising? In the absence of a third party, we must imagine one or both systems to possess some kind of additional effector-system, capable of physical action upon the environment, to be brought in automatically when goal-conflict arises. The simplest might be a destructive weapon of some sort deployed (presumably by each 'side') with the sub-goal of cutting the power to the other, or otherwise putting it out of action. Given a situation not too symmetrical, one system could then emerge triumphant and its primary goal would be attainable.

Suppose, however, that by chance or by design, the physical activity of one (or both) succeeded in *altering the goal-setting* of the other. Displaced in one direction, it would of course make matters worse; but if instead the displacement brought the two goal-settings *together*, then we would have the beginnings of a wholly different kind of 'resolution'. Instead of being rivals, the two systems could evidently become *partners*, sharing the effort of furthering the common goal. The closer the approximation of their respective settings, the greater the economy of total effort.

We can now take up the thread dropped at the end of the Introduction. Consider first the case where one of two systems (*A*) keeps its goal-settings totally isolated from outside influence. Here the only mutually viable alternative to deadlock would be the common pursuit of *A*'s goals. If, however, the other system (*B*), though not so isolated, has an inbuilt resistance to externally-imposed goal-changes (i.e. evaluates them negatively for feedback purposes) then beyond a certain point *B* may 'stick', and destructive tactics may again be the only way out of deadlock. A situation in which goal-adjustment is wholly one way is not fully 'social'. The 'adjusted' member is virtually an extension of the 'adjusting' member.

Consider next, however, the case where the two systems *A* and *B* are on an equal footing. Each is open to goal-adjustment, though each evaluates externally-imposed adjustment negatively for feedback purposes. Here a genuinely 'social' situation can develop. Each can pursue its goals only by taking into account the goals of the other, not only as facts about the world, but as potential members of its *own* goal-hierarchy. To the extent that *B*'s goal-directed activity can alter the goals of *A*, and vice versa, it may become impossible to attribute certain goals to *A* or *B* alone. The social unit formed of *A* + *B*-in-interaction becomes a goal-seeking system in its own right.

Clearly, in so far as *A* and *B* retain any individuality within such a system, it becomes advantageous for each to acquire advance information on the goal-structure of the other. If the end-result of interaction must be the mutual adjustment of goal-settings, then to prepare some adjustment in advance becomes a positively-evaluated achievement, by contrast with the negatively-evaluated status of externally enforced goal-change. The exchange of conventional representations of goal-structure ('opening their minds to one another') becomes an important social activity. Increasing smoothness of relationship (avoidance of deadlock and goal-conflict) can result from increasing ability to 'convey' (i.e. evoke states of readiness for) the outlines and details of the hierarchic structure of one another's organising system. Hence, of course, the importance of congruence between A's and B's basic goal-priorities, noted above. Without this, the process of 'touching-up' the recipient's state of readiness to match the originator's may have to be desperately indirect and cumbersome, if not impossible.

Once certain basic goal-settings have been approximated and social goal-pursuit has commenced, each individual will attach positive value to anything that brings the organising system of the other up to date, to match the current state of the field of activity. In short, one of the goals of each will be to *share information* with the other, bringing their respective 'maps' into agreement. Another will be to *share tricks or skills*. This means inducing the development of similar *organising sub-routines* in the two goal-complexes. Such sub-routines may simply organise external effector-action (as in tool-using, climbing, etc.); or they may concern the internal processes of calculation-in-view-of-ends (as in solving mathematical problems). In either case the organisers of sub-routines, once established, take their places among the 'conceptual building-bricks' in terms of which the individuals and the social unit form their images of the world.

When the number of members of a social unit increases beyond two, still another level of complexity opens up. If all could simultaneously adjust one another's goal-settings into conformity, no special problem would arise; but because of the serial nature of most communicative processes, what emerges is a self-organizing system with *internal delays*. Such systems are notoriously hard to keep stable. Even with only two members, the familiar example of two people trying to give way to one another on a narrow street shows the insidious power of a time-lag to frustrate mutual adjustment. In a large social unit, complete symmetry is out of the question. However similar the members may be initially, the problems of organising goal-compatibility require some members to take on different roles from others if the whole is to form a stable system. Hierarchic ordering (i.e. asymmetry in relationships to prevent vicious closed loops and deadlocks from forming), and the central coordination of at least some goal-priorities, seem inescapable.

In such a large group, then, we find ourselves confronted with topological problems of second order. We began by thinking of a goal-seeking system as a pattern or network of interactive elements, which had to evolve an organising hierarchy in order to cope adequately with a world of hierarchically-ordered complexity. Considering the interaction of two such systems, we have traced the necessity for communication channels to develop between them to prevent deadlock or mutual destruction. The result of this is the formation of a social unit, with goals assignable to it rather than specifically to any member. When a large number of members are linked by communication channels in this way to form a goal-directed social network, we find ourselves in many senses back at Stage 1, contemplating (ruefully?) once again the necessity for hierarchic organisation.

There is, however, one fundamental difference. This time, the elements of the system are individuals capable of forming concepts of the system. The concepts they form, in so far as they affect their goal-complexes, are liable by the same token to affect the nature of the system — and so *to affect their own validity*.[22a]

We cannot, of course, conclude from this that any generalisation regarding a social unit can become true (or false) if enough members believe it is. What we can affirm, however, is that a generalisation of this sort cannot be promulgated without exchanging some of its scientific (*predictive*) status for an (implicitly or explicitly) *normative* one. Like the 'predictions' of an apprehensive back-seat driver, 'you'll be in the ditch in a minute', its semantic function is to inform, not future expectation, but present action.

We cannot pursue this topic here. I mention it only to warn against over-simple hopes of what scientific investigation can do to establish predictive 'facts' in this area.

CONCLUSION

We have driven our way up from the level of primitive goal-conflict to that of politics and social organisation, tracing along the way the mechanics of communicative processes as far as we could.

Have we done more than repeat in cumbrous terms the commonplaces of the psychologist and anthropologist, with which we have found ourselves making contact from time to time? I do not profess to know. I think the train of development of the present ideas has seemed at times to have a momentum of its own, suggesting that it might, if followed, lead to genuinely fresh insights into the nature of social organisation; and I am solaced by the thought that this was a task laid down for me as appropriate to the present occasion.

But I must confess that it seems to me early days to en-courage anthropologists to delve deeply into the theory of communication. It is the *approach* of the information theorist, rather than his theorems and jargon, that may conceivably at this stage have something to offer. My hope is that at least the 'flavour' of this approach may emerge clearly enough from the present paper to initiate a fruitful discussion.

CHAPTER 10

Linguistic and Non-Linguistic
"Understanding" of Linguistic Tokens*

FOREWORD

During the summer of 1963, four symposia comprising a Working Session in Mathematical Biology were held at the RAND Corporation. The author participated in one of these symposia, concerned specifically with questions of "computer comprehension of language." The following short paper was prepared as a basis for discussion. The five participants in the symposium later co-authored a separate Memorandum presenting some results of the discussion and their conclusions.†

The present paper explores the distinction between recognizing an utterance, on the one hand, as a "symptom" of the state of affairs in or confronting its originator and, on the other hand, as a linguistic tool. It is suggested that, although only the first kind of understanding is required to enable a computer to accept data and answer questions in verbal form, such ability is no guarantee of its comprehension of all aspects of language. To attain full linguistic comprehension, the programme must also embody at least a "skeleton representation" of the linguistic context in which an utterance originates and from which it derives its linguistic significance as a goal-directed operator. By use of this richer model of its situation, a computer should be enabled to meet more sensitive tests of linguistic comprehension.

* Originally a RAND Memo., RM-3892-PR, April 1964.

† M. Kochen, D. M. MacKay, M. E. Maron, M. Scriven, and L. Uhr, *Computers and Comprehension*, The RAND Corporation.

The Inadequacy of a "Stimulus Equivalence" Model

There is no great difficulty in programming an artificial agent so that it classifies two sensory inputs as equivalent — so that the flashing of a lamp and the sounding of a bell, for example, evoke the same overt response or set up internally the same state of organization.

In trying to programme such an agent to handle human language intelligently, it is tempting to see the problem in similar terms — as one of securing "stimulus equivalence" between sensory stimuli, representing an object or a state of affairs, and linguistic stimuli representing the name of the object or state of affairs. The obvious objection to such a simple move, however, is that the reactions appropriate to perception of an object or a state of affairs are not always or even generally appropriate to perception of its mere name. We do not want our interlocutor to shake in his shoes every time he comes across the word "lion"!

Accordingly, as a second approximation, we might seek rather to secure stimulus equivalence between sensory stimuli, representing a state of affairs, and linguistic stimuli representing *assertions* of that state of affairs. An artificial agent would then be said to "understand language" if verbal assertions, such as, "The cat is on the mat," or, "This is a square," had an equivalent behavioural effect to that of an optical or other sensory presentation of the state of affairs described — either evoking appropriate response or contributing an appropriate item to its "cognitive map."

Without denying that a performance of this order would be adequate for many practical purposes, the aim of this brief paper is to show that it falls short of human understanding in a critical respect — but one that does not seem beyond mechanical remedy.

Perception versus Linguistic Understanding

As long as the linguistic assertions offered to an agent are true and unquestionable by definition, it is possible to miss or paper over the differences between perception of states of affairs and linguistic understanding of descriptions of them. Thus, in the simplest chess-playing programmes, no essential distinction can be made between the computer's "perceiving" the contents of (say) a chess-board by sensory means, and its "being told" them verbally. The author has even been assured by one designer that it made no difference to him or his machine whether the internally stored representation of the board was set up by an optical input via a "pattern-recognition" routine, or by a typewritten input in ordinary English via a "word-recognition" routine, or by direct feed-in from a suitable punched tape to the storage registers. These were all equivalent channels of communication between the board and the computer, and if the linguistic channel functioned successfully the computer must be admitted to "understand language." Any doubts on this score were to be dismissed as sheer "metaphysics."

At first sight there might seem to be a justification for this argument in certain human situations. A blind man, for example, may come to trust a human guide so implicitly that he virtually perceives through his guide's eyes, and the guide's words become barely perceived intermediaries in the channel of surrogate-visual communication. An aircraft pilot being talked-down in fog may be in a similar situation. Here we would agree that the sounds coming from the guide's mouth could, in principle. be replaced without loss by "bleeps" or other mechanically generated symptoms with the same indicative function, and the distinction between linguistic and non-linguistic understanding would evaporate.

All that this proves, however, is that for certain purposes an indicative linguistic form can have the same function as a non-linguistic symptom of the state of affairs indicated; it does not begin to prove the converse — that to understand an indicative utterance *means no more* than to react as to symptoms of the state of affairs denoted by it.

The issue becomes clearer when we consider cases in which the actual state of affairs is found *not* to correspond with what is asserted in an utterance.

THE INTENTIONAL CHARACTER OF LINGUISTIC UTTERANCE

Our senses normally enjoy at least as much confidence as our human interlocutors; yet our senses also can mislead us. When this happens we call it a distortion or an illusion, and explain it in terms of passive mechanical limitations or faults in our sensory apparatus. If a man says, "My eyes deceived me," we recognize the metaphorical usage, and do not impute any *motivation* to those organs. The same applies *a fortiori* if we are misled by symptoms from inanimate apparatus, or other physical clues, as when we say, "The fog deceived me into taking the Town Hall for the Post Office."

If a linguistic utterance turns out to have been misleading, we can of course take a similar attitude. If the blind man's guide says he is in the Post Office and he finds he is in the Town Hall, for example, he may simply ask, "*How* [i.e. by what causal sequence] has this situation arisen?" — just as if he had been using an inanimate blind-aid. In this case, however, there exists also a quite different kind of question: he may ask, "*Why* [i.e. for what purpose] did you say that?" This kind of reaction would be meaningless in relation to his eyes, or in relation to a television link, or any other "motiveless" collector of clues to his whereabouts. It points to an aspect of linguistic understanding which differentiates it from mere interpretation of symptoms. In a word, to perceive an utterance linguistically, rather than symptomatically, is to perceive it as *intentional* in form. Whether or not it be used as such on a particular occasion, a linguistic utterance is a *tool*. Language is not fully understood by any entity, whether natural or artificial, incapable of perceiving this aspect of it.

We can if we wish take this point in two stages. The word "lion," we say, *denotes* the creature. This denoting function is often taken as characteristic of a linguistic token, as distinct from a mere symptom, such as the smell of the lion, the sound of his roar, or the imprint of his paw. Well and good (at least in relation to objects). But how to explicate the notion of "denoting"? Inevitably, in the end we have to go back to the context for which linguistic tokens were invented — the situation in which one individual wants to adjust the "state of organization" of another, and uses combinations of tokens as tools to that end. Thus, although full linguistic understanding of an expression is possible without any reference to the intentions of a particular originator, one aspect of it will be beyond any entity incapable of understanding the concept of a tool, and what it means for the expression to be used as such.

Operationally, the notion of "intentional" here admits of mechanistic explication on the same lines as other notions related to "goal-directed," "purposeful" action — in terms of a "variational" criterion.[14,15,24] We define a state of affairs X as the aim or *goal* of an agent A, if A is so organized that any received indication of "mismatch," between the actual state of affairs (*say Y*) and X, would evoke a search for action (or preparations for action) calculated to reduce the mismatch.* By calling an *utterance* intentional, we imply that its form has been calculated with a view to a goal — namely, the determination of some aspect of the state of organization of some recipient (known or unknown).

For a recipient to be able to understand this intentional character (whether or not he attributes the intention to the current user), his information system must be equipped to represent not only the utterance and what it says, but also its functional significance — which implies the ability to represent it as something designed to be used by an originator, similar in linguistic repertoire to the receiver, to achieve a particular end. Without going into detail here,[9] it is clear that this requires internal activity over and above the filling out of a "cognitive

---

* If the aim were to avoid X, "reduce" in the foregoing sentence would be replaced by "increase," or "maintain above some minimum."

map" in accordance with what the utterance *says*, as if it were no different from the reading of some instruments. Complete linguistic comprehension will demand internal representation (at least in skeleton form) of the goal-directed feedback loop within which the utterance functions or could function — just as understanding of a hammer as a tool (and not merely a lump of matter) would demand some skeleton representation of its function. In either case, of course, the recipient's own goal-pursuing mechanism could serve as a representational surrogate.

Understanding the *use* of an expression by a particular individual in particular circumstances still more clearly requires the system to be capable of modelling the originator as goal-directed, especially if the utterance is directed to the recipient. (One operational implication, for example, will be that if a recipient *R*, having correctly perceived the intended function of an utterance by originator *O*, were not to conform to *O*'s intention as perceived, *R*'s system should be to some extent prepared for *O* to initiate corrective action, or in some other way — now or in the future — to evince the frustration of his intention (see Chapters 7 and 8).

Symptoms versus Descriptions

A further objection may however be raised to our line of argument. If the originator, though human, can be treated as a physical system, surely once his goal-directing networks have been taken into account there is no difference in principle between the evaluation of his linguistic utterances as clues to the state of affairs giving rise to them, and the evaluation of the performance of some non-linguistic channel, such as a fire alarm, or a barking dog, or a television system? In each case there may be distorting factors to be discovered and allowed for; after all, even a TV channel may reverse black and white!

It can be conceded at once that the linguistic output of an originator whose goals and behaviour pattern are known and stable could in principle be treated thus: simply as a succession of *symptoms* of the state of affairs, internal and external, that gives rise to them, from which the inference to that state could proceed on the same principle as from any other causally coupled symptoms (ringing bells, barking dogs, or spots of light on a TV screen). Our argument has not been that this is impossible, but simply that it leaves out an essential aspect of *linguistic* understanding. It is precisely the difference between treating an utterance as a *symptom*, and recognizing it as an intended *description* of a state of affairs, which differentiates most clearly the non-linguistic from the linguistic aspects of human communication.

In the special case of dialogue, however, there is a still stronger answer. The significant feature of dialogue between two agents who understand language in its intentional aspect is (as we have indicated) that in principle the goal-settings of an originator may *not* be treated as (all) fixed — for his goal strategy will in general depend from moment to moment on the way in which the recipient responds to his utterance. We have, in short, a situation of potential *goal-conflict*. If sufficiently symmetrical, it may in principle preclude either party from acquiring a full mechanical specification of the other, since the mutual backcoupling can systematically invalidate the attempt on either side (see Chapters 9 and 13).

In such reciprocal interactions, then, we can say categorically that a complete analysis of utterances as symptoms would be logically impossible for the interlocutor (though not necessarily for a detached onlooker with access to their internal workings). When we speak of the linguistic understanding revealed by human beings in such situations, therefore, we are clearly talking about something else, for which mere interpretation of symptoms does not in this case offer a live alternative.

CONCLUSIONS

Our main aim has been to show the operational reality of a distinction, often vaguely alleged, between the level of "understanding of language" required in a device for the mere acceptance and emission of information in verbal form, and the understanding of language enjoyed by human beings.

Our conclusion, however, is not that artificial agents must be incapable of understanding language in the fuller human sense. On the contrary, we have glimpsed what seem to be key features of the necessary mechanism, and the possibilities opened up are richly interesting enough to be explored in more detail elsewhere.

What seems clear, however, is that computer programmes for "language comprehension" which embody no perception of its intentional aspects do not show an understanding of language in the full sense that human beings do, and that without certain additional capabilities — notably the ability to embody a skeleton representation of the goal-directedness of their interlocutor and his aims in using words — they cannot fully do so. It is equally clear that, for many limited but important practical purposes, they need not.

CHAPTER 11

Comprehension of Utterances — Some Concluding Notes*

Utterances are exchanged between agents as a means of: (*a*) initiating, modifying, or confirming one another's actions (overt or internal) or conditional readiness for action; (*b*) evoking emotional or other experiences. The target of an utterance may be: (*a*) the recipient's "*map*" of the world (i.e. what he reckons with as fact or possibility in planning and executing action); (*b*) the recipient's *normative* system which determines the conditional priorities of various norms and goals, and actions directed thereto; (*c*) the recipient's (or just the originator's) sensory-aesthetic or other systems not directly concerned in the organisation of action adaptive to the external world (e.g. certain aspects of poetic utterance, etc.).

The *meaning* of an utterance (intended, standard, or received) can be defined as its selective function (intended, standard, or actual) on the range of possible states of the appropriate system. Thus, meaning is defined as a relationship, not an absolute property. An utterance is *meaningless* if it has *no selective function* (for one reason or another) on the appropriate range. We have to distinguish between meaninglessness due to: (*a*) lack of definition of selective function (e.g. nonsense syllables); (*b*) absence of the appropriate range in recipient (e.g. "colour" to a blind man); (*c*) incompatibility of two

---

* Originally an Appendix (by D. M. MacKay) to "Computers and Comprehension," RAND Memo. R.M.-4065-PR, April 1964, by M. Kochen, D. M. MacKay, M. E. Maron, M. Scriven, and L. Uhr.

or more components of the selective operator (e.g. "the milk is isosceles").

Clearly, utterances can be *partially* meaningful (or meaningless) under the above heads.

In this framework, *misunderstanding* can be defined as *discrepancy* between intended or standard and received selective functions. Note, however, that this is the *passive* sense of misunderstanding (e.g. "a misunderstanding exists") rather than the active sense (e.g. "you are misunderstanding me"). To misunderstand is to perceive an utterance as calling for an adjustment of organization discrepant with that intended or purported.

The last sentence emphasizes that the effort to understand an utterance is an effort to match the recipient in some sense to the originator; i.e. it presupposes an intention in the originator and an awareness (explicit or implicit) of this by the recipient. We must beware of any behavioural tests of understanding which omit to test for this.

An utterance as understood by a recipient has two distinct aspects — its *form* and its *weight.*

The first determines the form that the recipient's organizing system would assume if the utterance were fully accepted; i.e. if the selective operator it defines were fully applied to the organizing system.

The second determines the actual degree of coupling between the internal representation of this selective operator in the recipient, and his organizing system.

We thus picture the receipt of an utterance as a two-stage process, somewhat like the construction of a patch-board followed by the decision to plug it in — but different in that the final coupling need not be all-or-none.

In these terms, we can briefly characterize the understanding of a variety of utterances.

(*a*) A *statement* is aimed at the recipient's map-making system. Its received weight (the extent to which it is *allowed* to determine the form of the map) depends on the recipient's evaluation of the originator's goal in uttering it and of his reliability as a source (e.g. he may ask, " Is he trying to deceive me?" — "Does he have access to necessary data?").

(*b*) A *command* is aimed primarily at the recipient's normative system. It is calculated to secure action of a given form by altering the goal-priorities, rather than by mere physical reflex stimulation, of the recipient. Its perception as a command requires recognition that the recipient is in principle under feedback from the originator, with equilibrium dependent on his taking the required action. Its weight depends on the extent to which disequilibrium here is negatively valued (i.e. to ask, "What if I were to disobey?" would be relevant).

(*c*) A *request* differs from a command in relying for its weight upon the positive value (to the recipient) of satisfying the originator, rather than evoking mere negative avoidance of disequilibrium with him.

(*d*) A *question* is aimed formally* at updating the *originator's* own organizing system, by way of the recipient. Questions may be regarded as requests (or commands according to their form or tone) to construct a linguistic tool with the specified updating function. Their weight is thus derived in an analogous manner to that of requests and commands, with the added consideration that for many people the updating of others is a positively-valued activity in any case.

(*e*) An *instruction* differs from a command in specifying not an action or a goal, but a programme, whose goal may be only conditionally named, if at all (e.g. "To reach the house, drive five miles north on route 1, then two miles east on route 50").

(*f*) A *warning* is aimed at the recipient's normative system by way of his map. It presupposes a coupling (usually negative) be-

---

* Examination questions merely require the recipient to answer *as if* the examiner needed to be updated,

tween the internal representation of what the warning indicates and the evaluatory system which determines goal-priorities (e.g. an air-raid warning). Its effective weight depends both on the strength of this coupling and on the recipient's evaluation of the motivation and reliability of the originator.

(*g*) *Advice*, in general, may include instructions and warnings. It is characterized, however, by the implicit or explicit conditional, "If I were in your place ..." The weight claimed by advice thus depends on the extent to which its originator believes himself to have adopted the recipient's goal-structure, etc., when constructing it. The weight actually given it by the recipient will then obviously be calculated from his evidence on this point, as well as from the intelligence, knowledge, etc., he attributes to the adviser.

(*h*) A *promise* is aimed at the recipient's map of the originator's goal-settings. It indicates not only that the originator shares the recipient's goal named in the promise, but also that he recognizes himself in principle to be under feedback to the recipient in this connection (as in the case of commands).

As argued in Chapter 8, all utterances also have an indicative function, whether or not they are conventionally aimed at the recipient's cognitive map. Thus even a question or a command indicates implicitly certain presuppositions on the part of its originator. Understanding of these indicative aspects may be symptomatic or linguistic or both, and need not coincide with understanding of the conventional (interrogative, imperative, or other) aspect. A question such as "How long have you lived in Mexico?", for example (addressed to someone who never has), can be indicatively understood and replied to appropriately, even though it is interrogatively nonsensical.

CHAPTER 12

Generators of Information*

FOREWORD

This paper and the following one represent something of a digression, and for this reason find themselves at the end of the collection, out of chronological order. In the first we are back in 1952, wrestling with the relation between information and noise and considering in what circumstances events determined (in part) by random noise might be said to generate information. In the second, written by request on a similar topic eleven years later, the main emphasis is on a new point. Over and above any indeterminacy due to physical randomness, it is argued that interlocutors in dialogue have an irreducible logical indeterminacy for themselves and for each other. This would give their behaviour an irreducible selective information-content for one another even if their brains were as physically determinate as clockwork.

INFORMATION AND NOISE

The communication engineer is normally concerned with 'information on the move'. He takes his stochastic processes as they come, and his task is to map them on to a receiving field as efficiently as possible.

In this paper our attention will move one stage farther back, to inquire into the conditions under which information may be said to arise, and to discuss in particular the kinds of

* *Communication Theory,* W. Jackson (ed.), Academic Press, New York, 1953, 475–85 (copyright Academic Press).

mechanism that could produce 'original' information in the same sense as a human being is said sometimes to do.

Any question of this kind is bedevilled by the multiplicity of complementary senses in which the term 'information' can be used. From the standpoint of information theory, information is defined, in general, as that which causes or logically validates representational activity — activity in which a structure, purporting to represent something else, is produced or augmented.

This operational definition admits of as many subdivisions as there are distinct classes of representational activity. The reader is referred to the explanatory glossary (Appendix) prepared for a previous symposium for a fuller discussion of the resulting terminology. Here it must suffice to remind ourselves that correspondingly different measures of amount-of-information or information-content offer themselves according to the aspect of representational activity considered. If we are interested in the actual form and content (the so-called semantic aspects), the indices of metron-content and logon-content are relevant. If only the unexpectedness of the activity is of interest irrespective of its semantic significance, then it is the minuteness of the selection made from the ensemble of expected possibilities which is taken as an operational index of information-content. This, under the varying names of 'selective information-content', 'selective entropy', 'negentropy', or even simply 'entropy', is the important 'bulk measure' of information-content used in current communication theory; and it is this measure that we shall have in mind in what follows. By adopting it we imply that we regard the representational activity in which we are interested as a succession of selective operations on an ensemble of possible representations. Since in fact we shall be concerned with symbolic (or pseudo-symbolic) activity, this standpoint is appropriate.

A final caveat may be entered against the linguistic error of confounding 'information' itself with one or another of these measures of 'information-content'. To do so brings the same retribution as would the confounding of 'electricity' with 'voltage' or 'amperage'.

Since the notions of noise and randomness will be pivotal in later discussion, it may be provident now to seek to clarify their relationship to the notions of information theory.

The communication engineer, being concerned ultimately with the faithful reproduction of a message, measures its information-content by its mathematical unexpectedness. If, therefore, he is asked to reproduce a given 'white-noise' or 'random' signal that he knows to be equally likely to select any one of the ensemble of possible states of his channel, and thus to place the greatest demand on his channel capacity, he will estimate such a signal to have the greatest selective information-content for him per unit of time, irrespective of its apparent senselessness. However senseless a signal may seem, he is always politely ready to believe that it has operational significance for the ultimate receiver, i.e. that it represents some selective operator on the ultimate receiver's ensemble of significant representations. This does not of course mean that the receiver in fact carries out selective operations of corresponding magnitude, but only that he could do so if the signal were a member of some optimal ensemble of code signals agreed upon with the transmitter. In short, the selective information-content of a signal for a receiver has no direct connection with that for the communication engineer responsible for its passage.

On the other hand, any noise produced in the channel itself counts as negative selective information, because it is pre-empting part of the selective power of the channel and leaving only a residue for the desired signal. In fact, the badly phrased question, 'Is noise information?' exemplifies well the need for 'semantic hygiene' in this field. The question is incomplete. If translated, 'Has noise selective power?' it invites the immediate rejoinder, 'On what ensemble?' To specify the ensemble then removes all the ambiguity and obviates empty debate.

Implicit in the estimation of information-content in terms of selective power there lies a further assumption of communication theory, namely that knowledge of the code is free information for the receiver. To forget this is to invite apparent paradox. For example, if one out of a row of eight equiprobable letters ABCDEFGH is selected for me by 'successive halving' (as, e.g. C would be selected by 'left', 'right', 'left'), it is commonly assumed that I am left with only three bits of information. But I was able to interpret 'left' 'right' 'left' as C only because I knew also the order in which the eight letters were arranged. I shall need more than three bits of channel capacity to transmit this information to someone else, unless I am sure that he has set up an ensemble of letters in the same order.

These considerations are of course a commonplace of practical communication, but are sometimes forgotten when attempts are made to measure 'information-content' in other contexts. The general point is that even the utterance of a single two-valued proposition represents two selective operations:

(1) The choice as to which proposition to assert or deny.
(2) The choice to assert or deny it.

Communication has been effected, and information is meaningful, only in so far as both selective operations have been performed by the receiver.

SOURCES OF INFORMATION

What, then, constitutes a 'source of information'? We have seen that any stochastic process which somebody wants to reproduce elsewhere makes demands on the information capacity of the engineer's channel, and is thus, by his definition, an information source in a technical sense. It is a source of surprise. If we accept the definition of information as that which logically validates representational activity, it is undeniable that even a noise generator or a random number generator is a source of information in such a case.

Our instinctive objection to this statement reflects the fact that in such a case no agreed code exists according to which the noise signals could induce us to make any selective operations on an ensemble of significant representations, in particular on the ensemble of our own possible responses. In effect we want to distinguish between signals with surprise value and signals with meaning. It may be a pity that communication theory has attached the notion of information so exclusively to the element of surprise, though the engineer can hardly be blamed for assuming the meaningfulness (to someone or other) of what comes to his transmitter. One might perhaps try to rigorize usage by drawing the following distinctions: (*a*) a noise generator, like any unpredicted sequence of events, is a source not primarily of information, but, if we must call it a source of something, simply of surprise; (*b*) it becomes a source of information if and in so far as it leads to representational activity, and its 'output of information' is to be measured relatively to the ensemble of representations on which it evokes selective operations; (*c*) a source does not, however, produce significant information unless the representational activity evoked has significance for some receiver.

Thus, for example, a classical monkey on a teletypewriter would probably make heavier demands on channel capacity than a human user; representational activity would certainly occur at the receiving teleprinter, and in a technical sense 'information has been transmitted'. But because the classical monkey sends sequences of letters normally devoid of any agreed selective function for a human receiver, the latter could without contradiction state that he received no significant information from them. His private representation of 'that which is the case' has not been significantly altered.

In short, selective information-content does not measure a 'stuff' like water, or electric charge, but a relation (selective power) between a signal and a particular ensemble of representational acts of response. '*S* is a source of information' is thus an incomplete sentence. It must always be completed (even if sometimes implicitly) in the form, '*S* is a source of information to receiver *R*'.

Classifying a few typical stochastic processes under these headings, we may regard atomic disintegrations, valve noise, Brownian movements, random number generators, and the like, as 'sources of information' only in the technical sense. They are not normally (except perhaps in experiments of the 'table-turning' type!) generators of significant information.

A source of significant information, as we have seen, must be capable of embodying and abiding by an agreed code or symbolic calculus. Can we conceive of a mechanism capable of generating (and not merely reproducing) significant information in this way? Such must now be our inquiry, which may perhaps cast some interesting sidelights on the corresponding processes in the human being.

Concept-Handling Artefacts

We are familiar in these days with artefacts* such as digital computers which are capable of handling suitably coded logical data, and performing logical deductions. Such artefacts abide by an agreed symbolic code, and it is natural to ask whether they are not sources of significant information of the type we are seeking. Unfortunately, the strict logician would correctly maintain that such computing devices are merely transducers of information supplied to them by their users, and that since their output could in principle be predicted completely in advance, they generate no selective information whatever.

We might plead that unless we carry out the predictions we may well be surprised by their output, and in fact receive a great deal of information. This may be conceded. In fact a computer designed for example to play chess might be considered to engage in meaningful dialogue with a human opponent. As long as its choices were all logically determined uniquely by its data, however, it would be generating no selective information, but only reflecting back to its opponent the logical implications of the information it received as to his last move. It would, as we say, 'show no originality'.

Now we have seen that a noise generator can be regarded as a source of completely original but meaningless information. A logical computer *per contra* provides completely unoriginal but rigorously meaningful information.

---

* In the sense of 'artificial contructs', used to escape the associations of the word 'machine'.

It is natural to ask next whether one could not somehow combine devices of the two kinds in such a way as to generate processes at once original and meaningful. Two broad divisions of possible policy are apparent. (*a*) We may use noise generators to perturb selected functions of a deterministic logical artefact, or (*b*) we may devise an artefact whose elements function statistically, with an inherent but limited indeterminacy. While the two classes of artefact so devised could be made behaviourally equivalent, we may note in passing that there are important philosophical distinctions between them, which need not detain us here.

It is not proposed to discuss class (*a*) in detail. Some of the possibilities of making intelligent use of 'noise' in an artefact designed to take account of both structural and metrical aspects of information (in the semantic sense) have already been outlined by the author.[11] (Paper hereafter referred to as CDA.*) The thesis has since been developed in more general terms along the lines of (*b*).[14,15]

The crucial feature of artefacts in both the above classes is the introduction of metastable elements having effectively a variable probability of excitation governed by an input (preferably, though not essentially, a continuously-variable quantity such as bias-voltage, chemical concentration, or the like) that is in general quite separate from the normal excitatory input. Thus in class (*a*), the introduction of random perturbations of 'threshold' (e.g. by superimposing noise on the variable cathode-potential of a thyratron) can cause the probability of excitation in response to a given signal to vary smoothly between 0 and 1 as the mean threshold level is raised and lowered. In class (*b*), elements would be used whose responses to a given signal depended on internally fluctuating parameters of state, as well as on an adjustable bias-level, so that again the range of the latter would cover all possibilities from the complete inhibition of response to the generation of spontaneous activity at an adjustable frequency.

Details of mechanism need not here concern us. The basic point is that if an artefact is equipped to receive and handle and respond to information which is incomplete, by adjusting the relative probabilities of spontaneous changes of state of its internal representations according to the probabilities implicit

* Relevant portions of this outline (originally circulated in mimeographed form) were reproduced as an appendix to the paper presented at the Symposium.

in its information, then its activity, while not normally unreasonable, will frequently be unpredictable in a sense as fundamental as we care to make it by our choice of 'noise source.'

If, then, the artefact is equipped to handle meaningful symbols according to the rules of normal syntax, its reactions to a human interlocutor in the field of discussion so symbolized may frequently amount to the generation of new information — new ideas, for example, tentatively advanced, yet normally possessing finite chances of meaningfulness by virtue of the guiding probability configurations under which they have originated.

It may be helpful to compare this process with Shannon's statistical method of approximating to English sentences.[31,33] By arranging that the relative probabilities of his choices of English words reflected the statistical structure of spoken English, he was able to secure a high probability that a random method of choice would produce meaningful English sequences. Our artefact in effect uses the same method for 'disciplining' spontaneous activity into 'making sense', but has as its statistical guide the totality of its current and stored informational input. Its output thus promises not merely meaningfulness but relevance to the dialogue in process.

CODE-GENERATING ARTEFACTS

Thus far our artefacts have had no responsibility for the code in which their discourse is framed. Their concepts are those which we have equipped them to symbolize. We may reasonably reserve from them such admiration as we might accord an original thinker, until we are convinced that an artefact could originate not only new ideas in terms of old concepts, but new concepts *ab initio*.

We must once again be content with only a brief outline of ideas presented in more detail elsewhere;[14,15] but mention of the basic principle will doubtless suggest all the more interesting possibilities readily enough.

The key to the design of mechanisms capable of forming their own symbols is the possibility of valuative feed-back on transition probabilities. As this is also a possible key to all analogous problems of self-organization, one may perhaps be forgiven for elucidating it in terms of a simple model, originally constructed to illustrate some points made in CDA. This model has of course no pretensions to animal status, and justifies its existence solely as an explanatory device.

The model, illustrated in the figure, is made up of three identical units (the number is unrestricted in principle) each comprising a thyratron V which can actuate an electro-magnetic gate G so as to drop a ball-bearing from an aperture A over a two-pan balance B. B is mechanically linked to a potentiometer P, which governs the bias on thyratron V. The anodes of all thyratrons are supplied from a common capacitor C charged through a resistor R.

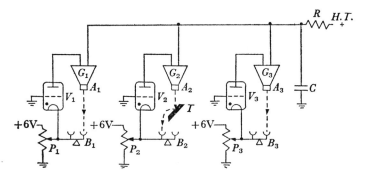

Fig. 1.   A simple probabilistic artefact illustrating valuative feed-back on probabilities of excitation

If now C is allowed to charge slowly, the thyratron with the lowest effective bias, say V_n, will tend to fire first, discharging C and releasing a ball from A_n. Normally this will fall into the right-hand pan of B_n, causing P_n to rotate and increase the bias on V_n. Thus the normal effect of a thyratron's firing is to reduce the probability of its firing next time.

If, however, a target T is placed under A_n so as to deflect any balls from A_n into the left-hand pan of B_n, the opposite effect will occur. The success of the model in striking the target when V_n fires will increase the probability that it will use V_n next time.

Evidently, no matter how the biases on different V's are set initially, the model will tend to an equilibrium state in which only the thyratron V_n fires and T is always hit. If moreover we move T to a new position, m say, the model will gradually 'unlearn' its original 'set' and eventually will be found firing only V_m.

In this example randomness is introduced only by the fluctuations of the thresholds of the various thyratrons, and the 'valuational feed-back' is quantized and rather inflexible. It illustrates even so the basic principle, whereby an artefact alters the transition probabilities governing its own activities according to its experience of their relative success (judged by some general criterion) and diminishes by a kind of 'natural selection' the probabilities of all except those which have been successful often enough.

Extensions of the principle in all directions will now be obvious, and only one need be mentioned. If in practice the target T is not stationary, but moves about from position to position in a stationary time series, it is easy to arrange the feed-back system so that the relative probability of firing of the nth thyratron V_n tends automatically to equal the relative frequency with which T is in position n. The artefact is not now playing an 'optimum game', but it has in effect made a symbol for an abstraction, namely the first-order statistical structure of the time series of positions of T.

Such a symbol is not indeed recognizable as a code group of impulses, but is constituted by the configuration of thresholds of the V_n. In quite a literal sense, the artefact is symbolizing its (statistical) expectation of what T will do next.

Along lines such as these one can envisage an artefact capable of forming internal 'symbols' for any regularity in the flux of its experience, by adapting its 'state of readiness' to match the regularity. The symbols are in fact the threshold configurations responsible for its readiness to make the corresponding matching responses, and, as we have seen, it is possible for an artefact to 'grope its way' towards the formation of such configurations, if necessary 'from scratch'.

The process would of course be greatly accelerated by even a modicum of instruction such as a child is given; and if the symbols are to correspond to communicable ideas, such instruction (i.e. valuative feed-back from an external interlocutor) would be almost indispensable. The point remains, however, that such a probabilistic artefact would always have the power of 'noticing' (preparing a symbolic state of readiness for) a new regularity never before named; and the regularity so symbolized need not always be an abstraction from the flux of incoming data, but may represent the outcome of some spontaneous internal sequence of trial and error at the cónceptual level.

Perhaps enough has now been said to justify the following summary:

(1) An artefact can be envisaged in which activities are of two types, (*a*) actions (internal or external), (*b*) adjustments of probabilities of actions. By valuative feed-back the results of (*a*) can evoke (*b*) so that the 'state of readiness' of the artefact — the total transition-probability-matrix (or t.p.m.) — forms in effect a representation of those regularities of its experience to which it has successfully responded.

(2) Such an artefact can not only generate information spontaneously, but can also form symbols for new concepts exemplified either in the flux of its incoming data or in the train of its internal spontaneous activity. In either case the probability of meaningless or unprofitable activity would seem in principle to admit of indefinite and automatic reduction.

(3) While all information is thus stored on a long-term basis in the form of the threshold configuration determining a t.p.m., the running symbols of a current 'train of thought' will of course be the trains of internal activity (at one or more levels) governed by the corresponding t.p.m.'s.

Human Information-Generators

The sidelong glance which we now cast on human processes of thought must be very tentative. We naturally feel inclined to ask whether human originality may not depend in part on random physiological processes disciplined in a comparable way by the t.p.m. of experience.

At the time when CDA was written, the digital computer was in popular vogue as an analogue of the brain (despite the protests of most physiologists) and an emphasis on the importance of randomness was unpopular among theorizers. Whether their opposition was stirred more by the mathematical or the metaphysical inconvenience of such considerations is doubtful, but in any case the evidence now seems overwhelming that neural processes could occasionally be subject to significant perturbation by random fluctuations in metabolism and other factors, particularly at any 'switch-points' where the thresholds for each of two or more alternatives were nearly equal.

Such perturbations will not in general produce surprising effects, since equality of two thresholds should ideally mean equal reasonableness for either alternative. They will, however, generate choices not prescribed uniquely by the data, and hence make essentially new contributions to the directions of corresponding mental processes.

We must, however, retain a reasonable perspective. It seems likely that the bulk of human discourse is not in fact unpredictable in principle, though this does not prevent us from describing it as an exchange of information. As usual, we measure the informational output of a speaker relative to the prior ignorance of the receiver. We can, however, remove this relativity by postulating an ideal observer who knows all the input information that has been received by the speaker, and all the transformations (in so far as they are physically determined) that this information will have undergone in him.

Such an observer, if the human speaker were a perfectly determined machine, would never be surprised by anything he said. For the ideal observer, this hypothetical speaker would not in fact be an information source.

If therefore we accept a physiological basis for thought processes (however little we understand them), we can distinguish two senses in which a human being can be described as an information source, with two fundamentally different physical correlates.

In perhaps the bulk of his discourse, he acts essentially as a transducer of information received from outside, from others, or from the abundant information source of the world of physical events. He can then be described as only a secondary source of information.

We can, however, recognize a second, if rarer, eventuality arising whenever input data do not completely determine output. The consequences of even a small perturbation may then be incalculably magnified; yet as we have seen the result will in general be both intelligible and novel in a fundamental sense. The human being is then unquestionably acting as a primary information source in the technical sense of the term.

Conclusion

There is no need to extrapolate this conclusion into some speculative form. In our abysmal ignorance with regard to creative thought-processes, we are probably obscuring at this moment the most vital features that we may eventually see to be 'obvious' in them. We may well content ourselves in summary with the more healthy permissive statement, that at least one physical process can be envisaged through which the brain, viewed as a physical system, could generate fundamentally original information. This is of course no more an explanation of such originality than the Uncertainty Principle is of the timing of spontaneous atomic disintegrations. It might perhaps yield as much enhanced an understanding of what we call 'randomness' as of the 'originality' that we link with it. The one clear fact is that we have only the faintest conception of the real nature of either.

CHAPTER 13

Indeterminacy, Uncertainty and Information-Content*

INDETERMINACY VERSUS UNPREDICTABILITY

To be invited to tackle an unexpected subject is sometimes frustrating, always challenging. In the present instance it was wholly gratifying; for although 'information' is often defined as what removes 'uncertainty', the interpretation of various 'uncertainty principles' in terms of information theory remains more than a little obscure; and the exercise of digging at the obscurity should be healthy.

It may be as well to begin with a basic distinction, between *indeterminacy* and *unpredictability*. To predict the behaviour of a large and complex mechanical system we require to programme a computer (artificial or otherwise) which must in turn be large enough to take account of all significant interactions between parts of the system. It takes little imagination to realize that in quite a small system (a cupful of water molecules, for example) we might find a complexity beyond the capacity of the largest imaginable computer, even if all the necessary data could be collected. The detailed behaviour of such a system could thus be termed 'irreducibly unpredictable'. To say this, however, is quite different from saying

* Paper read at the Stuttgart Congress on Information Theory, April 5th 1963. See foreword to Chap. 12. *NTZ-Communications Journal*, 3, 1964, 99–101.

that the system is 'indeterminate'. A determinate system may be defined as one for whose every future state *there exists now a completely determining formula* in the relevant calculus, whether or not the relevant initial conditions can be ascertained and the necessary computing operations carried out. If they can not, then the system is *determinate, but unpredictable.* Most large-scale situations as envisaged in classical physics were of this kind.

To describe a system as *indeterminate* is to imply not only that it is unpredictable, but (much more strongly) that *there exists no determining formula* whereby future state-descriptions are completely and necessarily implied by present data. In this case knowledge of initial conditions is not, even in principle, equivalent to certain knowledge of future states of the system.

UNCERTAINTY AND INFORMATION-CONTENT

When data D leave an individual I uncertain of a future event E, we measure the uncertainty-to-I of E by the weighted mean, $H = \Sigma\ p_i \log (1/p_i)$, of the logarithmic improbability, $\log (1/p_i)$, of each form of E envisaged as compatible with D. We then say that any fresh datum that changes the uncertainty H 'conveys information' (positive or negative) to I. The maximum change would result if E were uniquely *identified* or *selected* from the range of forms envisaged (hence the term 'selective information-content' often applied to H, to distinguish it from 'structural' measures based on analysis of the form of E).

For our present purpose we pass by those situations in which I just happens to be ignorant of data that in principle could be available to him. Obviously, in that case, which is typical of human communication, the selective information-content of E for I depends directly on his ignorance, both of D and of the forms of E compatible with D.

What interests us now is the information-content of E when all possible prior data D would still leave its form in some measure undetermined.

Here the distinction between unpredictable and indeterminate events becomes important. A sufficiently complex yet determinate mechanism (a spun roulette wheel, or even a tossed coin, for example) may leave us irreducibly uncertain of its course. Yet a good Laplacean (ignoring Heisenberg for the moment) would hesitate to ascribe to the outcome any 'absolute' selective information-content, for he would attribute the finite value of H (for us) either to our ignorance of initial conditions or to our limited computing facilities. From a Laplacean point of view the outcome would have no more fundamental novelty than the result of computing π to 10^6 decimal places, whose 'uncertainty' (errors excepted) is purely relative to the recipient.

If, however, there are ever any events E such that *no formula exists* whereby prior data D uniquely determine the form of E, then the prior uncertainty of each E is absolute, and its occurrence has an irreducible selective information-content.

HEISENBERG UNCERTAINTY

The only candidate for such absolute status in physical science is the uncertainty expressed in Heisenberg's Principle, $\Delta E \, \Delta t \geq \frac{1}{2}h$. As is well known, this implies that an event whose energy is specified within a margin of uncertainty ΔE cannot be located in time with less uncertainty than $\Delta t = \dfrac{h}{2\Delta E}$ where h is Planck's Constant and Δ is a conventional measure of uncertainty related to standard deviation. This empirical theorem has two components — the mathematical 'Uncertainty Principle' of Fourier analysis, $\Delta \nu \cdot \Delta t \geq \frac{1}{2}$, and the empirical relation between quantum energy and frequency, $E = h\nu$.

Debate still rages as to the 'absolute' character of this uncertainty — i.e. as to whether we should ascribe it to 'indeterminacy' or merely 'unpredictability'. This boils down to the question whether energy must invariably be related to frequency by the formula $E = h\nu$ — which no one can tell. All we can say is that *within the calculus of quantum theory* (based on the indivisibility of the quantum h) no formula exists whereby prior physical data precisely determine the form of atomic events.

If we take the proportionality of energy and frequency to be absolute, we are bound to grant that each atomic event has an absolute minimum to its selective information-content. The most fully-informed observer could determine only a prior probability-distribution for the spatio-temporal form of the event in question. After the event he can determine another probability-distribution, which will generally be narrower. Standard formulae of information theory can then give a numerical value to the 'amount of information generated' in the event.

Thus, to take a simple example, if a spherical light-wave is attenuated until the energy in a given time-interval is reduced to a single quantum, the place of impact of the corresponding photon on a (spherical) receiving screen may be completely undetermined by prior physical data. Its prior probability-distribution is uniform. After impact, it can be determined with a precision limited in principle only by the finiteness of the range of interaction ρ between elementary particles — of the order of 10^{-13} cm. Hence, with respect to spatial location, the maximum selective information-content 'generated' (i.e. the maximum in principle attainable) is of the order

$$\log_2 (4\pi r^2/\pi\rho^2) \quad \text{or} \quad 2 (1 + \log_2 r/\rho).$$

Even if we allow the radius r to expand to the 'Einstein radius' of the universe, we find that r/ρ can rise only to the order of 2^{130}. This sets an upper limit (of a kind) to the spatial selective information-content of a single photon-impact, at somewhere between 260 and 270 bits.

It is not suggested that at this stage in science we shall serve much purpose by making such calculations. The example merely illustrates the point that in this context a direct and even quantitative relation can exist between indeterminacy and selective information-content.

Human Beings as Information Sources

We have said that Heisenberg uncertainty is the only candidate for 'absolute' status in physical science. This means that any physical mechanism coarse enough to be insignificantly affected by Heisenberg uncertainty can be considered as in principle predictable.

Now among the relatively coarse structures of the world (compared with the dimensions of an atom) are the bodies of human beings. We are accustomed to regard human beings as *sources* of information, in a sense which is traditionally little short of absolute. Human action, we say, is *free* — at least to some extent, on some occasions. Human beings 'choose' between alternatives, each of which must (if choosing is to have any meaning) be 'open' to them beforehand. But if the only absolute uncertainty known to physics is of the Heisenberg variety, what becomes of this traditional conception? Surely, we may be asked, a human being can no more be a source of information (in any irreducible sense) than a cash register?

In answer to this, some people would question whether human bodies are in fact subject to the same physical laws as the rest of the material world. In our present state of ignorance, no conclusive evidence exists either to support or refute this suggestion. I shall argue, however, that it is unnecessary for its purpose; for we shall see that the actions of human beings can in fact have an irreducible indeterminacy, and hence selective information-content, even though their bodies were as mechanical as clockwork.

A Non-Existence Theorem

It will be recalled that we defined a system as determinate if for every future state there existed already a completely determining formula. By the same token we may define a future event as determined if there exists in the common calculus a complete description of it which is already definitive and binding on all — whether or not anybody in fact knows it or believes it. We shall now see that for the future decisions of human beings, curiously enough, *no such definitive description would exist in the common calculus,* even if the human brain and body were as mechanical as clockwork.[22,24]

To see this, we first observe that any complete description of a human agent must describe, at least by implication, *what he believes.* It follows that if the agent were himself to believe the description, it could not be valid *both* before *and* after his believing it. If valid before, then it describes the agent as not believing it, and so would become invalid if he were to believe it. If, however, it were preadjusted so that when believed by the agent it would become a correct description, then *ipso facto* it could not be a correct description beforehand. In neither case has the purported description any logical claim on the agent; for in the first case he is manifestly in error if he believes it, since it will then be false; while in the second he is manifestly not in error if he disbelieves it, since it is and will remain false unless he believes it.

Regardless of the mechanism of their bodies, therefore, human beings are *necessarily impossible of complete future-tense description in terms definitive and binding upon all.*

Suppose now that a human being A has to make a decision at time t (in the future). If his brain and environment form a rigidly interconnected mechanical system, then for a totally detached observer the description of all future brain-events, including those at time t, would be already implicit (*ex hypothesi*) in the present total state-description, and would therefore have no irreducible selective information-content for that observer.

For A, on the other hand, the observer's arguments, leading to detailed descriptions (predictions) of future brain-events, are *systematically invalid,* if we assume that any change in A's knowledge implies a corresponding change in A's brain-state. The data presupposed in the observer's arguments cannot claim to have absolute validity regardless of whether or not A

believes them, since (*ex hypothesi*) they imply a description of what *A* believes. To 'take a decision' is (by definition) incompatible with knowing (or believing one knows) the outcome already with certainty. Deciding and believing are here mutually exclusive.

Hence for the agent *A*, the prior uncertainty of the outcome at time *t* is absolute. It is not that there are some data which he needs, but of which he happens to be ignorant; it is rather that for him the crucial observations which enable the detached observer to complete his prediction *are not data*: they would not be valid were he (*A*) to believe them.

CONTRAST WITH UNCERTAINTY DUE TO IGNORANCE

In order to make this unique situation clear, we may contrast it with that of, say, the astronomer who wishes to predict the motions of some heavenly body, but lacks the necessary data. Here once again we can imagine an ideal isolated observer to whom all necessary data are available, so that all future state-descriptions are implicit in his present state-description. In this case, however, there is no disputing that (discounting relativistic corrections) the observations of the isolated observer *are valid data* for the astronomer, of which he just happens to be ignorant. Were he to believe them, he would be correct, and could in principle complete his prediction. Thus his uncertainty of the astronomical outcome is not absolute, and is radically different from the indeterminacy (to him) of his future decisions. In taking decisions he is not merely entitled, but logically obliged, to regard them as undetermined (in the sense we have been using); for he would be demonstrably in error if he did not.

It can of course be objected that we have oversimplified the astronomer's situation; for in the last analysis his brain is part of the universe that he is trying to predict, so that the events in his brain (including those when his knowledge changes) must be considered to have some slight effect upon every other part of the universe, including the heavenly bodies whose motions he wants to predict. This point is in fact cogently argued by Popper[27] in a classic paper. While I do not wish to minimize its philosophical interest, I would, however, emphasize the irrelevance of this extremely marginal indeterminacy to the issue before us. For the changes (if any) caused in a heavenly body when the astronomer's knowledge changes are conceptually incidental, in the sense that one could at least imagine without self-contradiction a shielding process which could intervene between his brain and the objects of his observation, so as to reduce the interference to any desired extent. The link we have assumed between the agent's beliefs and the states of his brain, on the other hand, is not of this character. These are rather two sides of the same coin — two aspects of one complex situation — so that a significant change in knowledge or belief is inseparably expressed and betokened by a significant change in brain-state.

DIALOGUE

So far, it may be objected, we have proved only that a human being is a source of information to himself. We have in fact allowed that to a completely isolated but fully-informed observer of his brain and environment (if such were possible) his actions could in principle be predictable and devoid of selective information-content. What then of his fellows with whom he engages in dialogue? Can he in any absolute sense be an information-source for them?

Indeed he can. For in genuine dialogue between two or more agents, the reciprocal interaction between them is such that for purposes of predictive analysis they become effectively one system (See Chapter 9). It follows that each agent in dialogue becomes unspecifiable in complete detail not only to himself, but to his interlocutors as well. In the common calculus to which all subscribe, *no formula exists* which validly specifies in complete detail the future state of any of them. To borrow a metaphor from quantum physics, there are 'interaction terms' which remove any possibility that one member of the dialogue could fully specify another, or be specified by him, as a determinate system. Once again, it is important to see that this is not a matter of 'ignorance' on the part of the members of the dialogue, as if valid determining formulae existed but they could not discover them. Even if our hypothetical 'fully-informed observer' wanted to relieve their uncertainty, he would inevitably discover that at the crucial points he had *no information to give them*. For them, any belief in his key observations would be self-refuting, nonsensical.

The absence of determining formulae for human actions in the common calculus is thus not an accidental inadequacy, to be remedied (in principle) by adding new terms. It is rather the reflection of a stubborn fact about our human situation. So far from being in error to regard one another as 'absolute' sources of information in dialogue, it is clear that we should be absolutely in error to do otherwise.

Conclusion

Our conclusion is thus that two kinds of 'absolute' uncertainty beset human knowledge. One is our uncertainty of microphysical atomic behaviour, due to the finiteness of the quantum of action inseparable from observation. At this level of detail it would seem that atomic events have for us an irreducible (potential) selective information-content.

The second type of 'absolute' uncertainty attends our knowledge of one another in interpersonal dialogue (as distinct from detached physical observation). Quite independent of any physical indeterminacy of our brain-mechanisms, this uncertainty reflects the fact that, in the public calculus of two or more persons in dialogue, *no valid definitive prediction exists* for their detailed future behaviour. In this relationship the action of each has an irreducible (potential) selective information-content, for his fellows as well as for himself.

Our habit of regarding one another as sources of information in dialogue is thus well founded; for the freedom we attribute to each other is not a matter of convention, but a matter of fact.

The Nomenclature of Information Theory*

(1) What Information Theory is About

SUMMARY. In everyday speech we say we have received Information, when we know something that we did not know before: when 'what we know' has changed. If then we were able to *measure* 'what we know', we could talk meaningfully about the *amount* of information we have received, in terms of the measurable change it has caused. This would be invaluable in assessing and comparing the *efficiency* of methods of gaining or communicating information.

Information Theory is concerned with this problem of measuring changes in knowledge. Its key is the fact that we can *represent* what we know by means of pictures, sentences, models, or the like. When we receive information, it causes a change in the symbolic picture or representation which we would use to depict what we know. It is found that changes in representations can be measured; so 'amount of information', actually in more than one sense, can be given numerical meaning. It is as if we had discovered how to talk quantitatively about *size*, through discovering its effects on measuring apparatus. We should at once find that it had the quite different but complementary senses of *volume*, *area*, and *length* — if not others. The analogy is potentially misleading, but may show us what to expect.

* From Proceedings of First London Symposium on Information Theory, 1950. Reproduced in *Proc. 8th Conf. on Cybernetics* (H. von Foerster, ed.), Josiah Macy Jr. Foundation, New York, 1951.

INFORMATION AS SOMETHING MEASURABLE? A hundred years ago it would have been thought merely a pardonable error if a stranger were to suppose 'information' to mean something *measurable*, like energy for example. 'Amount of information', or 'information-content', he would be told, is a metaphorical term, and has no numerical properties. But in fact he would not have been wrong; though he would have been in grave danger of confusion unless he learned to distinguish between a number of complementary senses of the term.

We might profitably compare the stranger's position with that of a man who has never heard of the concept of 'size'. He discovers that, in at least one sense of the term, a man, a sack of potatoes, an oildrum, and a tree-stump can all be said to have 'the same size'. He has now made some progress. At least, he knows that 'size' can *not* mean any of the properties which are not common to all four examples. With patience, he might eventually arrive at the notion of size by a process of elimination. He might even discover the different senses of the term, and coin the terms 'volumetric size' or 'volume', 'superficial size' or 'area', and 'linear size' or 'length', to distinguish three of its important senses.

But he has also a second line of approach which is more fruitful. He asks us: 'What *differences* does "size" make in an object? In what circumstances do you become aware of it? To *what* does size make a difference?' He discovers that we define the size (volume, area, etc.) of a body in terms of its ability to cause changes of a certain kind, in certain circumstances (for example, the indication of a point on a scale, as a result of certain well-defined operations with appropriate *measuring apparatus*). This is his clue. By systematically studying what happens when something is *affected* by the size of an object, he discovers the meaning of the term.

Our task is a similar one. We shall find it profitable to ask: 'To what does information make a difference? What are its effects?' This will lead us to an 'operational' definition covering all senses of the term, which we can then examine in detail for measurable properties.

Representations

In everyday language we say we have received information, *when we know something now that we did not know before.* If we are exceptionally honest, or a philosopher, we assert only that we now *believe something to be the case* which we did not previously believe to be the case. Information makes a difference to *what we believe to be the case.* It is always information *about* something. Its effect is to change, in one way or another, the total of 'all that is the case' for us. This rather obvious statement is the key to the definition of information. For those to whom 'metaphysics' is a bad word, any aura of metaphysical abstruseness which it may have is easily exorcised. What we know or believe, in science at least, could in principle be represented in a variety of quite precise ways: we might make a long statement, or draw a symbolic picture, or make a physical model, or send a communication-signal. All the results could in a sense show or embody what we believe: they are what we may call *representations*: structures which have at least some *abstract features in common* with something else that they purport to represent. These abstract features of representations are what we want to isolate. They form the real currency of scientific intercourse, which is normally obscured in wrappings of adventitious detail.

Now that we have established this fundamental notion of a representation, information can be described as what we depend on for making statements or other representations. More precisely, we may define information in general as that which *justifies representational activity.*

Criteria of 'Amount of Information'

Right at the start the term 'Amount of Information' or 'Information-Content' takes on two different kinds of meaning in answer really to different kinds of question. An example will illustrate the point. Two people *A* and *B* are listening for a signal which they know will be either a dot or a dash. A dash arrives. *A* makes various measurements, represents what has happened by a graph, and asserts that there was 'a good deal of information' in the signal. *B* says 'I knew it would be either a dot or a dash. All I had to do was to print one or other of these prefabricated representations. I gained little information.'

A and *B* are not of course in disagreement. For lack of a vocabulary, they are using the term 'amount of information' as a measure of different things. *A* is using the term in the sense of what we may call Scientific or Descriptive information-content. This in itself has two aspects, relating roughly to the number of independently variable features (structural information-content) and the precision or reliability (metrical information-content) of the representation he has made. The knowledge which he says has increased is knowledge of what has actually happened and been observed.

What of *B*? He was not waiting to observe everything that happened. He already knew that *for his purposes* only two kinds of representation would be needed, and he had prefabricated one of each. The knowledge he acquired was knowledge of *which representation to select*. *B* was therefore using 'information' in the sense of 'that which determines choice', and estimating what we may call *selective information-content*.

One word which was unexpected would have for *B* more selective information-content than a whole message which he was already sure he would receive.

A's approach is typical of the physicist, who wants to make a representation of physical events which he must not prejudge. *B*'s is typical of the communication engineer, whose task is to make a representation, at the end of a communication channel, of something he already knows to be one member of a set of standard representations which he possesses. His concern is therefore not with the size or form of a representation, but with its relative rarity, since this will govern the complexity of the 'filing system' he should use to identify it.

Each however may on occasion find both approaches relevant to different aspects of his work.

To sum up, if we ask how much information there is in a given representation, we may mean: 'How many distinct features has it? How many elementary events does it describe?' in which case we require answers in terms of *Scientific* or *Descriptive* information-content; or we may be ignoring questions of the size and complexity of the representation, and thinking instead of the complexity of the selection process by which it was identified, meaning: 'How unexpected was it? How small a proportion of all representations is of this form? In how many steps were you able to identify it in your "filing cabinet" of possibilities?' In this case our question refers to *Selective* information-content. Rarity here is the touchstone, as against logical structure in the first case. It will be realised — and this may be an important help to the understanding of the subject — that the term 'information' means something quite distinct from 'meaning'. If the reader begins by divorcing the two completely, he may find it easier to trace the connections in any subsequent reunion.

Our purpose in the explanatory glossary which follows is to see how the terms which have arisen in these different connections are related and to remove any possible misconception that these complementary senses of the term information-content are in any way competitive. The following diagram may help to keep the most important distinctions in mind.

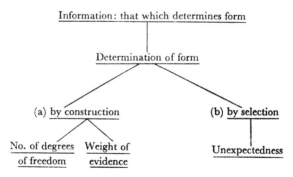

Information: that which determines form

Determination of form

(a) by construction   (b) by selection

No. of degrees   Weight of   Unexpectedness
of freedom   evidence

(2) *Explanatory Glossary*

1. THE SCOPE OF INFORMATION THEORY

Representations

1.1 Information Theory is concerned with the making of *representations* — i.e. symbolism in its most general sense.

1.1.1 By a representation is meant any structure (pattern, picture, model) whether abstract or concrete, of which the features purport to symbolize or correspond in some sense with those of some other structure.

1.1.2 The physical processes concerned in the formation or transformation of a representation are thus distinguished from other physical processes by the element of *significance* which they possess when conceived as representing something else.

1.1.3 For any given structure there may be several equivalent representations, defined as such through possessing certain abstract features in common.

1.2 It is these abstract features of representations which are of interest in Information Theory. Its aims are (*a*) to isolate from their particular contexts those abstract features of representations which can remain invariant under reformulation,* (*b*) to treat quantitatively the abstract features of processes by which representations are made, and (*c*) to give quantitative meanings to the several senses in which the notion of *amount* of information can be used.

1.3 The scope of Information Theory thus includes in principle at least three classes of activity:

---

* This aspect of the subject is already an established branch of mathematics under the name of Representation Theory or Abstract Group Theory.

Scientific or Descriptive Information Theory

1.3.1 Making a representation of some *physical* aspect of experience. This is the problem treated in *Scientific* or *Descriptive* Information-Theory.

1.3.2 Making a representation of some non-physical (mental or ideational) aspect of experience. This is at the moment outside our concern, being the problem of the Arts.

Communication Theory

Communication Channel

Space

1.3.3 Making a representation in one space *B*, of a *representation* already present in another space *A*. This is the problem of *Communication Theory*, *B* being termed the *receiving end* and *A* the *transmitting end* of a *Communication Channel*.

1.3.3.1 By a *space* is meant any physical or abstract mathematical coordinate frame-work or manifold, of any number of dimensions, in which the elements of a representation can be ordered.

1.4 These classes are not of course exclusive. The problem of communication in particular is seldom separable from one or both of the first two. In its present state of development Information Theory is concerned mainly with (1.3.1), the problem of representing the physical world, and (1.3.3), the problem of communicating representations (of any kind). It is communication theory (1.3.3), however, with its immense practical importance, which has received the greatest attention; and it is only the logical priority of the other two which prevents it from coming first on the list.

2. INFORMATION

Information

The foregoing definition of the scope of Information Theory provides the necessary background for the definition of *Information*.

2.1 In all its senses, the term can be covered by a general 'operational' definition (i.e. a definition in terms of what it *does*: as (e.g.) *force* is classically defined in terms of the acceleration which it causes or could cause). The effect of information is a *change* in a representational construct.

2.1.1 Information may be defined in the most general sense as *that which adds to a representation.*

2.2 This leaves open the possibility that information may be true or false.

2.2.1 When a representation alters, we define the new information as *true* if the change *increases* the extent of correspondence between the representation and the original.

2.2.2 The information is said to be *false* if the change *diminishes* the extent of this correspondence.

2.2.3 Strictly, the truth or falsehood is an attribute of the resultant representation, but it is customary to attribute it to that which has given rise to the change in the representation.

3. MEASUREMENT OF INFORMATION-CONTENT

Two quite different but complementary approaches are possible to the measurement of Information-Content, and have given rise to uses of the term in quite different senses.

3.1 From a quantitative analysis of what a representation *portrays*, we can isolate fundamental numerical features common to all its equivalent representations, and can say that they constitute the 'corpus of information' which it contains or represents.

3.1.1 'Information-Content' in this context is a numerical index (in one sense or another) of the 'size' of the representation itself.

3.2 But if instead of asking 'How many elements etc. are there in this representation?' we ask 'In how many stages, and in what way, has it been *built up*?' we arrive at a different kind of measure. This becomes clear if we consider that the same representation could be constructed in a number of different ways according to the amount of prefabrication used.

3.2.1 'Information-Content' in this context is a numerical index of the complexity of the *construction-process*.

3.3 In the following paragraphs, 4 and 5, these two approaches will be discussed. The first has given rise to two complementary definitions of what has been called 'amount of information', and the second approach to a third definition. These, however, are not rivals, but are autonomously valid measures, appropriate in answer to different questions.

4. ANALYSIS OF REPRESENTATIONS

4.0.1 Representations communicable in a two-valued (yes or no) form are necessarily *quantal* in structure, since an 'imperceptible change' in a two-valued logical form is by definition meaningless. All the *changes* are discrete, therefore the elementary concepts of logical representations are discrete and enumerable.

4.0.2 In fact a large class of such representations can be reduced to a form made up only of identical elements, so simple that their only attribute is *existence* (Wittgenstein, Ref. 40). This fact provides a basis for the quantitative analysis of such representations (MacKay, Ref. 11). (Representations not amenable to precise logical description have not so far been considered in the theory, though a large class of these might be handled in terms of approximate quantal equivalents representing 'upper and lower bounds' to their logical content.)

4.0.3 In general a pattern reduced to such fundamental terms will contain a certain number of distinguishable groups or clusters of elements, the elements in each group being indistinguishable among themselves. There are thus two numerical features of interest.

(1) The number of distinguishable *groups* or clusters of indistinguishable elements in a representation, and

(2) The number of *elements* in a given group or cluster.

4.0.3.1 The number of groups, and the numbers of their elements, may be thought of as respectively analogous to the number of columns and the number of entries per column in a histogram.

4.1 *Structural Information-Content*

4.1.1 The number of *distinguishable groups or clusters* in a representation — the number of definably independent respects in which it could vary — its *dimensionality* or *number of degrees of freedom* or *basal multiplicity* — is termed its *Structural Information-Content*.

Structural Information-Content

Logon

4.1.2 The unit of structural information, one *logon* (Gabor, Ref. 6; MacKay, Ref. 11), is that which enables one such new distinguishable group to be defined for a representation. Thus structural information is not concerned with the *number* of elements in a pattern, but with the possibility of *distinguishing between* them.

4.1.2.1 For example, if we are counting identical sheep jumping a gate, and we have no sense of time, our result can only be represented by a certain total number; but if we have a clock, we can now define what we mean by 'the number in the first minute' and 'in the second' and so forth, and represent our result by a set of *distinguishable* subtotals. The clock has provided *Structural* information. In a similar way the ability to distinguish (e.g.) spatial position along the gate would provide distinguishable subtotals and hence increase the structural information-content of our representation.

Logon-Content

4.1.3 *Logon-content* is a convenient term for the structural information-content or number of logons (number of independently variable features) in a representation (e.g. the number of independent coefficients required to specify a given waveform over a given period of time).

4.1.4 The number of logons provided by apparatus per unit of coordinate-space (centimetre,

Logon-Capacity (possible syn. logon-density)

square centimetre, second, etc.) is termed its *logon-capacity*.

4.1.4.1 For example, a channel whose bandwidth permits of l independent amplitude readings per second has a logon-capacity of l: in a microscope, logon-capacity is a measure of *resolving-power*; and so forth.

Structural Scale-Unit

4.1.5 The reciprocal of logon-capacity is termed the *structural scale-unit* for the apparatus.

4.2 *Metrical Information-Content*

Metrical Information-Content

4.2.1 The number of (indistinguishable) logical *elements* in a given group or in the total pattern is termed the *Metrical Information-Content* of the group or pattern.

Metron

4.2.2 The unit of metrical information, one *metron*, is defined as that which supplies one element for a pattern. Each element may be considered to represent one unit of evidence. Thus the amount of metrical information in a pattern measures the *weight of evidence* to which it is equivalent. Metrical information gives a pattern its weight or density — the 'stuff' out of which the 'structure' is formed.

4.2.3 In a scientific representation, each metrical unit may be thought of as associated with one elementary event of the sequence of physical events which the pattern represents.

Metron-Content (syn. metrical information-content)

4.2.4 Thus the amount of metrical information in a single logon, or its *metron-content*, can be thought of as the number of elementary events which have been subsumed under one head or 'condensed' to form it. For example, in the case of a numerical parameter, this is a measure of the *precision* with which it has been determined.

4.2.4.1 Notice that these elements are indistinguishable, so that their number is *not* the number of binary digits (5.1.3) to which the logon is equivalent.

4.2.5 When we come to represent the results of physical observations, we are often interested in magnitudes which are not directly proportional to the metron-content. The representations we use do not then show the metron-content explicitly. It must be clearly realised that metron-content as defined is a measure of the number of elements appearing when what is believed to have happened is represented *in its most fundamental physical terms*.

4.2.6 Thus if an estimate is made of a parameter from a statistical sample, the elementary events concerned are the arrivals of 'unit-contributions' to the sample. These could be represented by the number of intervals occupied

Conceptual Scale on a *conceptual scale* proportional to metron-content.

4.2.7 On the other hand, the usual representation shows the magnitude of the parameter concerned, and not generally the metron-content, on a linear scale, graduated in elementary intervals which in the useful limit are just large enough to give the representation of the magnitude (scale-reading) a probability

Proper-Scale of $\frac{1}{2}$. Such a scale is termed a *proper-scale*. Now the probable error, in a normal population, is inversely proportional to the square root of the size of the sample. Hence the magnitude in such a case would be shown as occupying on the proper scale a number of elementary intervals proportional only to the square root of the number of elementary events. The number of metrons is (in this special but common case) the square of the number of occupied intervals shown in this less fundamental physical representation.

Numerical Energy 4.2.7.1 In connection with radar information the term *numerical energy* has been used to represent what is essentially the metron-content of a signal. It is the ratio (Total energy)/(Noise-power per unit bandwidth).

4.2.8 In general then a clear distinction exists between (*a*) the fundamental representation on a conceptual scale showing the invariant number of logical elements, and (*b*) the representation of the magnitude which is of practical interest. In fact the connection between the two is little closer than that between the precision with which a given variable can be measured and its magnitude. Precision increases monotonically with metron-content, but few quantities are *linearly* related to metron-content. *Power* and *energy* in the classical case are among the few exceptions; this accords with their apparently fundamental status among physical concepts.

Scale-Unit

4.2.9 The *scale-unit* of a magnitude is the minimum interval in terms of which the scale can usefully or definably be graduated.

4.2.9.1 For a magnitude imprecisely known it is defined as above (4.2.7) to be equal to the probable range of error. A magnitude supported by a single metron occupies just one interval on such a scale. In practice, larger units are often used, e.g. range of standard error.

4.2.9.2 But it should be remembered that in *theoretical* representations the size of the scale-unit is generally limited by our inability to *define* a smaller unit in terms of the *coincidence-relations* out of which physical representations are constructed.

Coincidence-Relations

4.2.10 The number of metrons per unit of coordinate-space is termed the *metron-capacity* or *metron-density* of a physical observation-system (cf. 4.1.4).

Metron-Capacity (syn. metron-density)

4.2.11 The coordinate-interval over which one metron is acquired is termed a *conceptual unit* or (undesirably) a *metrical scale-unit* of coordinate.

Conceptual Unit Metrical Scale-Unit (undesirable syn.)

4.2.12 It will be noted that metron-content is necessarily positive.

4.2.13 Returning to the example of the jumping sheep, let us now suppose that we are trying to determine a figure for the average value of some parameter of a sheep, in each group which we are able to distinguish. Assuming for the sake of illustration that the parameter is normally distributed, the metron-content of each estimate would be proportional to the number of sheep per group, and the probable error in each estimate would be inversely proportional to the square root of this number. Hence the number of proper-scale-intervals occupied by the estimated parameter would be proportional to the square root of the metron-content of each group.

4.2.14 The term 'amount of information' in a sense analogous to this was first used by R. A. Fisher (Ref. 4), who defines it as follows: Suppose we have a probability distribution function $f(x, x_0)$ showing how in a given population a variable x is distributed about a parameter x_0, e.g. $f(x, x_0) = Ae^{-(x-x_0)^2/2\sigma^2}$. The 'amount of information' in n samples from the population is defined as n times the weighted mean of $(\partial \log f/ \partial x_0)^2$ over the range of x — i.e.

$$n \int_{-\infty}^{\infty} \left(\frac{\partial \log f}{\partial x_0}\right)^2 f \, dx.$$

Equivalent forms are

$$n \int_{-\infty}^{\infty} \frac{1}{f} \left(\frac{\partial f}{\partial x_0}\right)^2 dx \text{ and } - n \int_{-\infty}^{\infty} \left(\frac{\partial^2 \log f}{\partial x_0^2}\right) f \, dx.$$

In the case of a normal distribution, this reduces to the reciprocal of the variance, provided that the range is independent of x_0. It is thus a direct measure of precision, though it is not dimensionless unless suitably normalised.

4.3 *Representation of Descriptive Information-Content*
The Descriptive Information-Content of a given representation is specified by setting down the metron-content of each logon. This may be represented in various ways.

4.3.1 One convenient method is to use a multidimensional *information-vector* in an *information-space* of which each axis represents one logon. The squares of the components of this vector are the metron-contents of the respective logons. Thus the square of the length of the

Information-Vector
Information-Space

vector itself is the total metron-content, the sum of the individual metron-contents.

4.3.1.1 In this representation the angle between two directions has a direct interpretation as a measure of *relevance*. A dependent statement is defined by a ray in the space, and the metron-content afforded to it by the information is found by squaring the projection of the information-vector on the ray.

Relevance

4.3.1.2 A new *complete representation* may be set up by supplementing this dependent statement (4.3.1.1) by a set of others represented by orthogonal rays. This process amounts to a *rotation of axes*, which leaves us with a new total metron-content equal to the old.

4.3.2 The same processes can be represented in terms of matrix algebra, if the metron-contents of logons are set out initially as the elements of a diagonal *Information-Matrix*. Dependent statements now define vector functions, and their metron-content is found by forming scalar products of the form $\phi' \cdot I\phi$, where I is the information-matrix, ϕ a vector function, and ϕ' its transpose. Under all complete ('unitary') transformations, the *trace* or sum of the diagonal elements of I remains invariant, being the total metron-content.

Information-Matrix

Trace (syn. spur, characteristic, diagonal sum)

4.3.3 An alternative geometrical representation suitable for some particular cases employs a three-dimensional histogram having a coordinate and its Fourier-transform (e.g. time and frequency) as its two basal axes. Since the number of logons provided by given apparatus is proportional to the product of bandwidth (*q.v.*) and conjugate coordinate, the base is divisible into equal cells each representing one logon. On each cell is erected a column having a height proportional to the logarithm of metron-content. This gives the total *volume* of the histogram the same qualitative significance as the logarithm of the volume spanned by the information-vector of 4.3.1.

5. COMMUNICATION: REPLICATION OF REPRESENTATIONS

5.1 The problem of communication usually concerns representations of which all parts *exist already* in the past experience of the receiver. In other words the receiver already possesses prefabricated components of the representation.

5.1.1 In fact it is generally assumed to be known that the complete representation to be

Ensemble replicated is one member of a finite *ensemble* (*q.v.*) of possible originals, some of which have in the past been communicated more often than others. We may then say that these more common messages 'give less information' than the others, using the notion of 'information-content' now in the important sense of para. 3.2.1.

5.1.1.1 Our message is here thought of as telling us to *select* one prefabricated representation.

5.1.1.2 We are not now asking 'How big is it?' or 'How much detail has it?' but rather 'How unusual or unexpected is it?' or 'How much trouble will it take to find it in my ensemble?'

5.1.2 A convenient measure of information-content in this sense is the *negative logarithm* (*base* 2) *of the prior probability* of the representation concerned (Shannon, Ref. 31; Wiener, Ref. 39).

5.1.2.1 The base 2 is chosen because a selection among a set of n possibilities can be carried out most economically by dividing the total successively into halves, quarters, eighths, etc., until the desired member is identified. The number of stages in this process is then the integer nearest to, and not less than $\log_2 n$.

5.1.2.2 The information-measure so defined equals the *number of independent choices between equiprobable alternatives* which would have to be determined before the required representation could be identified in the ensemble of which it is a member. (The prior probability measures the fraction of the members of the ensemble which are of the required kind.)

5.1.2.3 This, like the first two measures (paras. 4.1.1 and 4.2.1), represents a number of logically "atomic" propositions; but this time they define, not the representation, but the selection-process leading to it.

5.1.3 Information-content in the above sense of *that which determines choice* may be termed *selective information content.*

Selective Information-Content

5.1.4 The *unit* of selective information-content, one *binary digit* or *bit*, is that which determines a single choice between equiprobable alternatives.

Binary Digit (syn. bit)

5.1.5 In a long sequence of different representations of which the ith kind has a prior probability p_i (and hence an average frequency of occurrence p_i), the average amount of selective information per representation is evidently the weighted mean of $-\log p$ over all kinds of representation, or $H = -\sum p_i \log p_i$, which apart from some ambiguity of sign in the literature is also the standard definition of the *entropy* of a selection.

Entropy

5.1.5.1 Where representations take the form of continuous functions, H takes the form $-\int f(x) \log f(x) \, dx$, where $f(x)$ is the probability distribution of the representative variable x. It is thus the weighted mean of $[-\log f]$ over the range of x.

5.1.6 In practice the receipt of a communication-signal disturbed by noise merely alters the form of $f(x)$ (generally narrowing it), and does not specify x uniquely. The amount of selective information received is then defined as the *difference* between the values of H computed before and after receipt of the signal.

5.1.7 When two representative variables, x and y say (discrete or continuous), are in question, knowledge of the value of one may affect the prior probability of the other. In the above notation, $f(y)$ depends on x, so that the entropy

Conditional Entropy

H of *y* will also vary with *x*. If we picture an ensemble in which values of *x* occur in their expected proportions, we define the *conditional entropy* of *y*, $H_x(y)$, as the average value of the entropy of *y* (calculated for each value of *x*) over all members of this ensemble.

5.1.7.1 This may also be described as the 'weighted mean entropy' of *y*, weighted by the probability of getting the different values of *x*. It therefore measures our uncertainty about *y* when we know *x*.

5.1.7.2 An analogous conditional entropy $H_y(x)$ can be defined for *x* when *y* is known.

Equivocation

5.1.8 Where *x* and *y* represent respectively the input and output of a noisy communication channel, the conditional entropy $H_y(x)$ is termed the *equivocation*. It is a measure of *ambiguity*.

Capacity

5.1.9 The number of bits per second which a channel can transmit is termed its *capacity*. For the case (5.1.8) it is defined as the maximum of $[H(x) - H_y(x)]$.

Relative Entropy

5.1.10 The ratio of the entropy of a source to the maximum value which it could have while using the same symbols is called its *relative entropy*.

Redundancy

5.1.10.1 *One minus the relative entropy* is termed the *redundancy*.

5.2 These considerations suggest a more economical method of communicating a representation.

5.2.1 Instead of transmitting a physical representation of the representation itself, we may transmit a representation of the *selection-process* by which it may be identified in the ensemble of possible representations which is assumed to exist at the receiving end.

Code-System

5.2.2 A system whereby a representation is defined by a selection-process is termed a *code-system*.

5.2.3 The corresponding representation of

Code-Signal

the selection-process transmitted is known as a *code-signal*.

5.2.3.1 As a physical sequence the code-signal will itself have metrical and structural features as discussed in para. 4, and will be definable by a vector in an information-space. But its structure need not have anything in common with that of the *representation* which it identifies.

5.2.3.2 On the other hand, the ordinary case of making physical representations *could* be thought of formally as a special case of coding, one-to-one.

5.3 It follows that the result of an experiment, as well as a communication-signal, could be anal-

Selective Information-Content of a Description

ysed in terms of its *selective information-content*.

5.3.1 This is a relative measure, depending on the number of distinct results which were regarded as equally probable by the observer. The result observed is thought of as specifying one of a number of possibilities already contemplated by the observer as forming an ensemble in defined proportions.

5.3.2 The amount of selective information derived from the experiment can then be computed in the same way as for a message (5.1).

5.4 The entropy or selective information-content of a selection should not be facilely identified with the physical entropy of thermodynamics. The two are equivalent only in the particular case where the ensemble from which the selection is made is a physical one defined for a state of thermodynamic equilibrium.

5.4.1 For example, if all n distinguishable voltage-levels of a transmitted signal are regarded as equiprobable, the selective information-content per logon is proportional to $\log n$. On the other hand, the physical entropy-increase is proportional to (or must exceed) n^2 (MacKay, Refs. 12 and 13).

5.4.2 Here the correlation is between *metrical* information-content (para. 4.2.7) and physical entropy-increase. In fact metron-content can be thought of here as the number of unit-increases of physical entropy — i.e., of elementary events — which have been subsumed under one head, thereby losing their distinguishability and potentiality of serving as 'bits'.

Alphabetical Index of Terms used in Information Theory and related Communication Theory. References are to Paragraphs in the Glossary.

Bandwidth
In general terms, the region of Fourier-space (*q.v.*) to which the output of an instrument is confined. In particular, the effective frequency-range (conjugate to a given coordinate) to which it responds.

Binary digit (5.1.3) Unit of selective information-content.

Bit Capacity (5.1.9) Number of bits transmissible per second.

Code-system (5.2.2)

Code-signal (5.2.3)

Conceptual unit (4.2.11) The coordinate-interval in which one metron is acquired. Reciprocal of metron-density.

Ensemble A set of possibilities each of which has a defined probability.

Entropy (5.1.5) (*a*) In statistical mechanics, k times the weighted mean of the (negative) logarithm of the probabilities of members of an ensemble. (*b*) In thermodynamics, that function of state of a body or system which increases by $\int_1^2 \Delta Q/T$ in a reversible process between two states 1 and 2, where ΔQ is the heat taken up by the body or system at temperature T. (Definitions (*a*) and (*b*) are equivalent.)

Conditional (5.1.6)

Relative (5.1.10)

Equivocation	(5.1.8)
Fourier-space	The space whose dimensions represent variables which are Fourier-transforms of coordinates (e.g. the frequency conjugate to the time coordinate).
Information **Information-** **content**	That which alters representations (2.1).
Metrical	(4.2) A measure of the weight of evidence in a representational pattern.
Selective	(5.1.3) A measure of the unforeseeableness of a representation.
Structural	(4.1) The number of independently variable features or degrees of freedom of a representation.
Information- **matrix**	A matrix in which the metrical (and structural) information-content of an experiment is specified.
Information- **space**	The space in which independent logons are represented by orthogonal rays, and their metron-contents by the squares of distances along these rays. (4.3.1)
Information- **vector**	The vector whose components in information-space are the distances just mentioned.
Logon	Unit of structural information-content ($q.v.$).
Logon-capacity **(poss. syn.** **Logon-density)**	(4.1.4) Number of logons per unit of coordinate space.
Logon-content **(syn. Structural** **Information-** **content)**	(4.1.3) Number of independently variable features.
Metron	(4.2.2) Unit of metrical information-content ($q.v.$).
Metron-capacity **(syn. Metron-** **density)**	(4.2.10) Cf. logon-capacity.
Metron-content **(syn. Metrical** **Information-** **content)**	(4.2.4) Measures the weight of evidence to which a representation is equivalent.

Numerical energy (4.2.7.1) Ratio of (Energy)/(Noise Power per unit bandwidth). A particular example of metron-content.

Proper-scale (4.2.6) A representational scale on which equal intervals are equiprobable.

Redundancy (5.1.10.1) One minus relative entropy.

Representation (1.1.) A symbolic picture, model, statement, etc.

Scale-unit (4.2.9) The minimum interval in terms of which a scale can definably or usefully be graduated.

Metrical (4.2.11) Undesirable equivalent of *conceptual unit*. Reciprocal of metron-density.

Structural (4.1.5) Reciprocal of logon-capacity.

(3) Postscript on
Structural Information-Content and Optical Resolution

(A) Extracts from Quantal Aspects of Scientific Information*

LOGON-CONTENT. It was Kant who said: "reason has insight only into that which it produces after a plan of its own." The design of an experiment is essentially the specification *a priori* of a pattern, of categories in terms of which alone the result can be described. All the events of the experiment must find a place in one or other of these, though of course not all categories will necessarily find an exemplar in a given experiment.

Since each independent category enables us to introduce a measure of differentiation — i.e. of form or structure — into our account of a result, we can regard knowledge thereof as providing us with *prior* or *structural information*. We can therefore define a unit of structural information, or (using Gabor's term[6]) a *logon*, as that which enables us to *formulate* one independent proposition, describing one independent feature of the result. (Whether when we have formulated the proposition we shall find any metrical information to give it logical content, is another matter.) The amount of structural information in a result, the *logon-content*, is thus the number of

* First published in *Philosophical Magazine*, 1950, **41**, pp. 289–311.

independent categories or degrees of freedom precisely definable in its description.

LOGON-CAPACITY.   In many cases structure is defined in terms of a reference-coordinate. For example the density-pattern on a photographic plate can be described by a function of one or more space-coordinates; and the structure of a telephone signal can be specified by a time function. The *logon-capacity* of an experimental method can in such cases be defined as the number of logons which it specifies per unit of coordinate-interval, or coordinate-space if several coordinates are involved. The total number of independent categories or features in the result is then the integral of the logon-capacity over the extent of coordinate-tract occupied.

Thus the logon-capacity of a microscope in a particular region in the focal plane can be defined in *logons/cm.²*, and measures the resolving-power in that region; for suitable test-objects a resolving power in a given direction can also be defined, in logons/cm. The logon-capacity of a galvanometer or a communication-channel is measured in logons per second, and represents the number of (practically) independent readings per second which can be made with the apparatus.

FREQUENCY-RESPONSE.   It is useful here to introduce the idea of frequency-response in a somewhat generalized form. With instruments measuring functions of time it is common practice to define performance in terms of the frequency-response of the instruments to sinusoidal inputs of different time-periodicities. In the same way one can define Fourier-variables associated with other coordinates, in order to assess the performance of other types of instruments.

For example one could use sinusoidal density-patterns of different *space*-periodicities to define the "frequency-response" of a microscope, if one may so extend the use of the term. In each case a precise meaning can be given to the *frequency-bandwidth* of an instrument, as the effective range of input-frequencies (i.e. of the Fourier-variable) to which it is sensitive.

(For example in a microscope this is a space-frequency range normally extending from zero to a value directly proportional to the aperture used. It thus measures the fineness of detail perceptible, in terms of a Fourier-type of analysis of the transparency-function which represents the object. One need hardly say that "frequency" here is quite distinct from the frequency of the light used.) It should be noted that with more than one coordinate the Fourier-variables must be represented in a Fourier-space in which "bandwidth" is defined by a "volume" not necessarily rectangular.*

BANDWIDTH AND LOGON-CAPACITY. The bandwidth of an instrument in the above sense is directly related to its logon-capacity. The relation arises from the well-known uncertainty-principle which can be written

$$\Delta f \cdot \Delta q \geq K_s \qquad (1)$$

where Δf represents the effective range of frequencies (conjugate to a coordinate q) to which the apparatus is sensitive, Δq twice the "uncertainty"† in q, and K_s a number which we may take to have the value $\frac{1}{2}$.

Equation (1) will now be justified from our present point of view. It means that points on the q-axis cannot be defined uniquely at closer intervals than $K_s/\Delta f$, so that the logon-capacity is $\Delta f/K_s$ or $2\,\Delta f$. To attempt to talk of "an interval smaller than Δq" would be to try to construct a logical pattern identical with that of "a frequency higher than Δf", which cannot by definition appear in any result and is therefore observationally meaningless. The logon-content l of an experiment involving a tract of extent q is thus:

$$l \leq q \cdot \Delta f/K_s \leq 2q \cdot \Delta f \qquad (2)$$

* The author is indebted to a correspondent for raising this point.
† I.e., Δq is the effective range of q.

Structurally-Defined Scale-Units

THE STRUCTURAL INFORMATION-AXIOM. In structural propositions the absolute magnitude of y is irrelevant. They are essentially definitions of propositional functions of which y is to be the argument. Accordingly the scale-unit of q can be defined only in terms of coincidence-relations independent of the magnitude of y. In the foregoing section we used the concept of bandwidth (generalized) to define a scale-unit Δq which was a property of the apparatus used, ascertainable beforehand by an independent experiment, and hence counting as prior information on subsequent occasions. The general relation (1) which we used then can be justified directly in terms of our initial axiom that only coincidence-relations or compounds thereof are valid as logical elements in scientific statements.

Let us consider then the case of a simple harmonic function of q, with periodicity f. It will be associated with definitive points on the q-axis, independent of amplitude, whenever the function crosses the axis, i.e. at intervals of half a period. (It is also arguable that ingenious experimentation should make it possible to define the quarter-period or the radian-period independently of amplitude.)

In any case, the scale of q is conceptually provided with a set of points at intervals of K_s/f, where K_s is of the order 1.

These points, however, are all logically indistinguishable, representing collectively a single fact — the accurate value of f. What we want is a set of uniquely identifiable points, to serve as labels. To single out desired points we must provide a comparison-pattern to act as a "pointer". For instance a frequency $f - \Delta f$ will produce a pattern coinciding with the first at intervals of $K_s/\Delta f$. If all values of Δf from zero can be observed, a continuous range of intervals from infinity down to $K_s/\Delta f$ can be observationally defined. The *structural scale-unit* of q, Δq, is thus $K_s/\Delta f$. Conversely, if Δq is an arbitrary interval, the number l of logons relating to it which can be formulated can be written as $l \leq \Delta q \cdot \Delta f / K_s$, since l is integral. Thus for a single logon $\Delta q \cdot \Delta f \geq K_s$ (equation (1)). (It should be remembered that in practice the terms "effective length" and "bandwidth" often have a slightly different numerical connotation from that here employed.)

RESOLVING-POWER. To illustrate these ideas we may examine the problem of optical resolving-power. As our purpose is only expository we shall consider the somewhat unrealistic case of a narrow rectangular aperture and an ideal object which can be represented by a transparency-function of only one coordinate, x say, parallel to the long edge of the aperture. The situation can then be represented by the two-dimensional diagram of Fig. 1. P is a point on the aperture, with coordinates (r, θ) relative to a point O on the object. Light is incident in the direction Oy. The problem has two parts. Firstly, we shall establish a relation between the

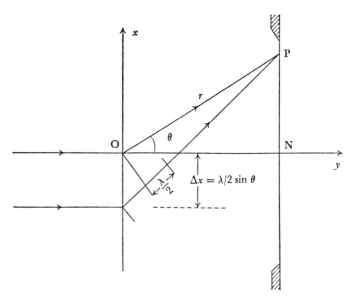

Fig. 1   Normal incidence.

position of P and the information gained through it about the object; and secondly, we can calculate the logon-capacity for a given type of aperture.

Suppose that light of wavelength λ is received through P. This makes it possible to distinguish logically points along the possible light paths to P at intervals of $\lambda/2$, so that, with centre P, we can give logical significance to a series of arcs of radii $n\lambda/2$, where n has integral values. These arcs will intersect the x-axis and establish coincidence-relations with the incident wavefront at intervals of $\lambda/2 \sin \theta$, in the vicinity of O. There is thus a correspondence between the point P and a space-function having a periodicity $f_x = (\sin \theta)/\lambda$ in the object. Indeed if the aperture is closed everywhere except at P and the pole, N, the pattern seen has just this periodicity.

This analysis has assumed that a plane wavefront was incident normally on the x-axis. If instead the light is incident in the xy plane at an angle ϕ to Ox (Fig. 2) the possible light-paths from P must be traced through the object to their origin on the incident wavefront; and the logically describable paths will be those whose *total* lengths are integral multiples of $\lambda/2$. The corresponding space-periodicity defined on the x-axis will then be $f_x = (1/\lambda)(\sin \theta + \sin \phi)$.

To calculate the logon-capacity we need only observe that the "bandwidth" is directly proportional to the range of $\sin \theta$. Thus if θ can have all values between $\pm \theta_m$, $\Delta f = (2/\lambda)$ $(\sin \theta_m)$, and the logon-capacity is $(4/\lambda)(\sin \theta_m)$ *logons per cm.*

This logon-capacity will not, however, be realized in the case of normal incidence, for then f_x is only $(1/\lambda) \sin \theta_m$, and only $(2/\lambda) \sin \theta_m$ points are specified on the x-axis. Only by increasing ϕ to θ_m can the full resolving-power be achieved. Increasing ϕ beyond this value, to give so-called "dark-ground illumination", will increase f_x but not Δf. The number of logons per cm. will not be increased, though owing to the removal of background light the visibility of detail is generally improved.

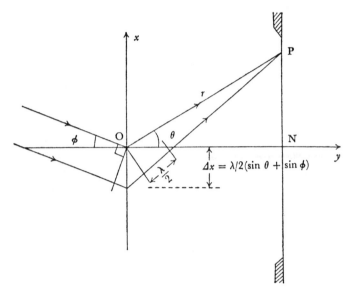

Fig. 2   Incidence at angle ϕ.

(B)   *The Structural Information-Capacity of Optical Instruments**

INTRODUCTION

In the theory of communication much use is made of the well-known "sampling theorem" (Gabor, Ref. 6; Shannon, Ref. 31) of Fourier analysis which states that a function restricted to a frequency bandwidth W/sec may be specified uniquely by $2W$ equally-spaced samples per second. This is

* *Information and Control*, Academic Press Inc., 1958, **1**, pp. 148–52. (Copyright Academic Press Inc.)

usually interpreted as implying that such a signal of duration T has $2TW$ degrees of freedom (called "logons" by Gabor). The number of degrees of freedom is taken to be proportional to the area of "Fourier-space" occupied.

In the theory of optical resolving power the same ideas can be used without apparent difficulty in the case of a one-dimensional aperture, where aperture-width takes the place of bandwidth, and object-length the place of time-duration (MacKay, Ref. 11). Once again the number of degrees of freedom appears to be proportional to the area of Fourier-space occupied.

When, however, one considers a two-dimensional aperture, an apparent paradox appears. Reasoning along the same lines, one finds the number of degrees of freedom or logon-content of an image to be proportional to the product of the number for each dimension, and hence to the area of the aperture (Gabor, Ref. 7; Toraldo di Francia, Ref. 37). This, however, would imply that a microscope with a line-aperture (e.g. a linear or annular slit of vanishingly small area), should have no re-solving-power; whereas it is easily verified that this is not the case.* As the width of a rectangular aperture is diminished to zero, the resolving-power in the corresponding direction becomes smaller and smaller; but resolution in the other direction is unaffected, and the total number of logons tends to a lower limit proportional to the width in that direction. With an annular aperture this fact is even more convincingly demonstrated. The apparent paradox has led some[7] to suggest that the signal-noise-ratio ought to be brought into the defini-tion of logon-content, while others (Good, Ref. 8) have sought to resolve it by using notions of one-to-one mapping to throw doubt on the present definition.

THE FORMULA FOR LOGON-CONTENT

I have suggested elsewhere[20] that the paradox may be simply resolved without recourse to such complications,

---

* Gabor, personal communication (1953).

for it is not a paradox but a mistake. The logon-content of a signal occupying bandwidth W and time T is not $2TW$, but $(2TW + 1)$, for the mean value offers one extra degree of freedom. Similarly with a one-dimensional optical aperture, of numerical aperture α and an image width X, the logon-content in di Francia's notation[37] should be $[(2\alpha X/\lambda) + 1]$ and not $2\alpha X/\lambda$. A rectangular aperture $\alpha \times \beta$ with an image $X \times Y$ gives a logon-content $[(2\alpha X/\lambda) + 1][(2\beta Y/\lambda) + 1]$ which tends to $[(2\alpha X/\lambda) + 1]$, and not to zero as β tends to zero*.

It is possible to reach this conclusion in another way by considering the number of logically-discriminable points in the field of view. In the early paper referred to[11] the author showed that this was $(2\alpha X/\lambda)$ in the one-dimensional case, but unfortunately perpetrated the same mistake as the communication engineer by identifying the logon-content with this number instead of with $[(2\alpha X/\lambda) + 1]$. With wisdom after the event, it is obvious that a single logically-discriminable point divides a field into *two* logically-discriminable regions, so that the field then has not one but two descriptive degrees of freedom or logons. l_X logically-discriminable points divide the X-dimension into $(l_X + 1)$ discriminable regions; in the other direction l_Y logically-discriminable points divide the Y-dimension into $(l_Y + 1)$ regions. The result in the two-dimensional case is a logon-content of $(l_X + 1)(l_Y + 1)$.

The Relevance of Noise

The correction of this mistake would be a small matter were it not for the doubts which the apparent "paradox" has aroused about the validity of logon-content as an *a priori* measure of logical dimensionality. As mentioned earlier, the suggestion has been made, first that logon-content cannot be defined without reference to signal-noise ratio, and second, that "logical dimensionality" is indefinite because an *n*-

---

* In his recent book, *Science and Information Theory* (Academic Press Inc., New York, 1956, p. 97), L. Brillouin has given the correct expression for the logon-content, although without using the term.

dimensional function can be "mapped" into a space of fewer dimensions, without loss of "information."

There is of course one obvious truth in the first suggestion. If an instrument has a pass-band or aperture which does not have sharply defined margins, the effective bandwidth will depend upon the minimum signal-level which is detectable — or at least upon the minimum acceptable ratio of marginal to modal values of the transfer function. The conventional definition of "practically independent amplitudes" in such a case remains to be worked out. But in the common case of a "practically rectangular" transfer-function, as with a band-pass filter or a normal microscope-aperture, any ambiguity is purely marginal, and in no case affects the order of magnitude of the logon-capacity, in the way that would have been required had the "paradox" been a genuine one.

Re-mapping

The second suggestion, which has been recurrent since 1951 at least, [35] arises I think from a slight confusion. The basic idea of re-mapping can be pictured as the labelling of each point in one space, by a code-number indicating a corresponding point in another space. Thus an optical image made up of 100 independent patches of light, each having 10 possible intensities, would normally be describable as having a logical dimensionality or logon-content of 100. It would be identified by a point in a space of 100 dimensions, each having 10 discriminable coordinate-values. On the other hand, each point in this space could be labelled with a single number in the range $1-10^{100}$, so that the whole could be mapped on to a single dimension having 10^{100} discriminable coordinate-values.

Identification versus Reconstruction

Why then could not the original image be described as one-dimensional, with a logon-content of unity? The reason is quite simple. The logon-content of an image measures the dimensionality of the most economical prescription, not for *identifying* but for *constructing* it. Before the one-dimensional signal could be used for the reconstruction of the picture, it would have to be "decoded" — turned back into a prescription of precisely 100 independent intensities. Logon-content, then, is a genuine invariant, a property of the *relation-structure* of a signal, determining the minimum number of independent steps required for its *reconstruction*. Selective information-content, on the other hand — the logarithm of the number of discriminable points or cells in the descriptive space — is also an invariant, determining the minimum number of independent steps required for the identification or selection of a signal from the ensemble of possible signals. If the steps are binary, yes-or-no steps, the selective information-content of our optical image is then $\log_2 (10^{100})$ or $100 \log_2 10$. It is proportional to logon-content if all degrees of freedom have the same number of possible coordinate-values; but an increase in selective information-content by increasing the number of coordinate-values would do nothing to enhance logon-content or resolving power. It is indeed quite possible to adopt measures which increase selective information-content to the detriment of logon-content, giving a brighter picture with poorer resolution. This alone should make it clear that some measure of information other than selective information-content is relevant to the design of optical instruments.

Nothing that has been said precludes the possibility, indicated some years ago by the author[16] and others (Blanc-Lapierre, Ref. 2, Toraldo di Francia, Ref. 37) that an image distorted by an instrument of low resolving-power may be refined if prior knowledge of the image is available. Prior knowledge in effect reduces the independence of the components of the original, so that its effective number of degrees of freedom is reduced. There is then no paradox in the fact that the number of components in the refined image may exceed the logon-capacity of the instrument, since these components are not independent. A lucid discussion of the possibility has recently been given by Toraldo di Francia.[37]

Conclusions

This brief paper has had but two objects: to correct a small error which the author has shared in propagating, and to dispose of some misapprehensions regarding logon-content as an information-measure.

We have seen that if the logon-capacity of an instrument be defined as the number of logically-distinguishable *intervals* in the field of view, rather than the number of logically-definable *points*, this increases by 1 the usually accepted logon-capacity in each direction, so that an image $X \times Y$ transmitted through a rectangular aperture $\alpha \times \beta$ has a logon-capacity of $[(2\alpha X/\lambda) + 1] [(2\beta Y/\lambda) + 1]$. This disposes of the paradox that a linear aperture of negligible area gives a finite resolving-power.

The suggestion that signal-noise ratio be invoked in explanation is thus shown to be unnecessary, although when the transfer-function is non-rectangular one must consider amplitudes in determining "effective bandwidth". The idea that one-to-one mapping leaves dimensionality indefinite has been shown to rest on a confusion between the requirements for *reconstruction* and for *identification* of a signal. Logon-content measures the minimum dimensionality of the reconstruction-process. For the minimum complexity of a selection or identification-process, on the other hand, the appropriate measure is the familiar selective information-content; but this may be misleading if used uncritically as a criterion of optical performance.

References

Author's Note: These references are simply a collation of those in the original papers, and are not meant to be exhaustive.

1. Bar-Hillel, Y. and Carnap, R.: Semantic Information. In W. Jackson (Ed.), *Communication Theory.* London: Butterworths, 1953, p. 503.

2. Blanc-Lapierre, A.: Application to Optics of certain results and methods of Information Theory. In W. Jackson (Ed.), *Communication Theory.* London: Butterworths, 1953, p. 513.

3. Dixon, R. M. W.: *What is Language? — A new Approach to Linguistic Description.* London: Longmans Linguistics Library, 1965.

4. Fisher, R. A.: *The Design of Experiments.* Oliver and Boyd, 1935, p. 188.

5. Fodor, J. A. and Katz, J. J. (Eds.): *The Structure of Language.* Prentice-Hall, 1964.

6. Gabor, D.: Theory of Communication. *J. Inst. Elec. Engrs.,* 1946, **93**, III, p. 429.

7. ————: Optical Transmission. In *Information Theory: Third London Symposium,* E.C. Cherry (Ed.). London: Butterworths, 1956, pp. 26–33.

8. Good, I. J.: Discussion in *Information Theory: Third London Symposium,* E. C. Cherry (Ed.). London: Butterworths, 1956, p. 33.

9. Kochen, M., MacKay, D. M., Maron, M. E., Scriven, M. and Uhr, L.: *Computers and Comprehension.* RAND Memo. RM-4065, 1964.

10. Lorente de No, R.: Transmission of Impulses through Cranial Motor Nuclei. *J. Neurophysiol.,* 1939, **2**, p. 422.

11. MacKay, D. M.: On the combination of digital and analogical techniques in the design of analytical engines. 1949. Mimeographed. Reprinted as Appendix to *Mechanization of Thought Processes* (N.P.L. Symp. No. 10, 1958). London: H.M.S.O., 1959, pp. 37–52.

12. ———: Quantal Aspects of Scientific Information. *Phil. Mag.*, 1950, **41**, pp. 289–311.

13. ———: The Nomenclature of Information Theory; Quantal Aspects of Scientific Information; and Entropy, Time and Information. In *Proc. of Information-Theory Symp. London; Sept. 1950.* Lithoprinted Amer. Inst. Radio Engrs., 1953.

14. ———: Mindlike Behaviour in Artefacts. *Brit. J. Phil. of Sci.*, 1951, **II**, pp. 105–21; also 1953, **III**, pp. 352–53.

15. ———: Mentality in Machines. *Proc. Arist. Soc. Suppt.*, 1952, **XXVI**, pp. 61–86.

16. ———: Brit. Pat. Appln. 29315/48 (1948). Outlined in W. Jackson (Ed.), *Communication Theory*. London: Butterworths, 1952, p. 521.

17. ———: The Epistemological Problem for Automata. In C. E. Shannon and J. McCarthy (Eds.), *Automata Studies.* Princeton: Princeton University Press, 1955, pp. 235–51.

18. ———: Complementary Measures of Scientific Information-Content. *Methodos*, 1955, **VII**, pp. 63–90.

19. ———: Towards an Information-Flow Model of Human Behaviour. *Brit. J. Psychol.*, 1956, **47**, pp. 30–43.

20. ———: Discussion in *Information Theory: Third London Symposium*, E. C. Cherry (Ed.). London: Butterworths, 1956, p. 32.

21. ———: Operational Aspects of Intellect. In Proc. N.P.L. Conf. on *Mechanization of Thought Processes, 1958*. London: H.M.S.O., 1959, pp. 37–52.

22. ———: (*a*) Information Theory and Human Information Systems. *Impact of Science on Society*, 1957, **8**, pp. 86–101. (*b*) On the Logical Indeterminacy of a Free Choice. *Mind*, 1960, **69**, pp. 31–40.

23. ———: Information and Learning. In H. Billing (Ed.), *Learning Automata*. Munich: Oldenbourg, 1961, pp. 40–49.

24. ———: The Use of Behavioural Language to Refer to Mechanical Processes. *Brit. J. Phil. of Sci.*, 1962, **XIII**, pp. 89–103.

25. Mackay, D.M.: Cerebral Organization and the Conscious Control of Action. In J. C. Eccles (Ed.), *Brain and Conscious Experience*. New York: Springer-Verlag, 1966, pp. 422–45.

26. Miller, G. A.: The Magical Number 7 plus or minus 2. *Psychol. Rev.*, 1956, **63**, pp. 81–97.

27. Popper, K. R.: Indeterminism in Classical and Quantum Physics. *Brit. J. Phil. of Sci.*, 1950, **1**, 117–33 and 173–95.

28. Prior, M. and Prior, A.: Erotetic Logic. *Philos. Rev.*, 1955, **LXIV**, pp. 43–59.

29. Rosenblueth, A., Wiener, N. and Bigelow, J.: Behaviour, Purpose and Teleology. *Philosophy of Science*, 1943, **10**, pp. 18–24.

30. Russell, B.: *Logic and Knowledge* (especially "The Philosophy of Logical Atomism" (1918) and "Logical Atomism" (1924)). London: G. Allen and Unwin, 1956.

31. Shannon, C. E.: A Mathematical Theory of Communication. *Bell Syst. Tech. J.*, 1948, **27**, pp. 379–423; 623–656.

32. ———: Communication in the Presence of Noise. *Proc. I.R.E.*, 1949, **37**, pp. 10–21.

33. ———: Prediction and Entropy of Printed English. *Bell Syst. Tech. J.*, 1951, **30**, pp. 50–64.

34. ———: In H. von Foerster (Ed.), *Cybernetics*. Trans. of 8th Conf., Josiah Macy Jr. Foundation, New York, 1951, p. 219.

35. Shannon, C. E. *et al.*: In *Cybernetics, loc. cit.*, p. 195.

36. Shannon, C. E. and Weaver, W.: *The Mathematical Theory of Communication*. Illinois: University of Illinois Press, 1949.

37. Toraldo di Francia, G.: Resolving Power and Information. *J. Opt. Soc. Am.*, 1955, **45**, pp. 497–501.

38. Ullman, S.: *The Principles of Semantics*. Glasgow: Jackson, 1951.

39. Wiener, N.: *Cybernetics*. New York: John Wiley, 1948.

40. Wittgenstein, L.: *Philosophical Investigations*, trans. G. E. M. Anscombe. Oxford: Oxford University Press, 1953; 2nd Ed. 1958.

41. Yngve, V. H.: The Translation of Languages by Machine. In E. C. Cherry (Ed.), *Information Theory*. London: Butterworths, 1956, pp. 195–205.

Index*

Abstraction, hierarchy of, 53
Accuracy of measurement, limits to, 1, 178ff.
Actor-language, 58ff.
Adaptive matching-response, 51, *61–69*, 73, 112
Adaptive trial and error, 69, 72, 142
Advice, 131
Airy disc, 5
Ambiguities of visual perception, 69
Amount of information, measures of, 10, 42, 57, 158, *171–175*
Artifacts, probabilistic, 54, 140
Artificial language(s), 35, 81, 90, 109
Attention, 61
Atomic propositions, 2, 59, 81, 172

Bandwidth, 175, 178ff.
Bar-Hillel, Y., 81
Basic symbols, 51, 54, 61
Basic vectors, 48, 72
Binary digit, bit, 16, 172
Blanc-Lapierre, A., 188
Blind spots, epistemological, 113
Boltzmann, L., 57
Brain mechanisms, 23, 26, 63
Brillouin, L., 186

Capacity of channel, 15, 134, 173
Carnap, R., 81
Central nervous system, 63–66
Coding, 46, 173
Coincidence relations, 2, 168
Commands, 100, 130

Commitment, religious, 114
Communication, 20, 74, 96, *108*, 171
cross-cultural, 105
failure of, 111
system, 15, 171
untruthful, 29, 163
Complementarity, 1
Conditional entropy, 173
Conditional probabilities, 34, 62, 73
Conditional probability matrix (C.P.M.), 84, 95, 106
Conditional readiness (for behaviour), 22, 70
Consciousness, 53
Content-elements, 81
Content-measures, 81

Descriptive information-content, 12 15, 45, 59, 82, *159*
Dialogue, 126, 153

Eddington, A. S., 2, 17
Elementary events, 3, 160
Elementary symbols, 50
Entropy, 3, 57, 172
conditional, 173
relative, 173
thermodynamic, 16, 174
Ensemble
of possible messages, 57
of states of readiness, 71
Equivocation, 173
Evaluatory feedback, 67, 140ff.
Evidence, weight of, 49

* Page numbers printed in italics refer to definitions or explanations of terms.

Failure of communication, 111
Feed-back, evaluative, 67, 141
Fisher, R. A., 4, 5, 169
Fourier analysis, 184
Fourier-space, 185
Frequency-response, 179

Gabor, D., 4, 5, 165, 178, 184–185
Goal-complex, 106, 112
Goal-directed activity, 35, 60, *67*, *95*, 106
Goal-settings, hierarchy of, 90, 106
Good, I. J., 185

Heisenberg's Principle of Uncertainty, 1, 148
Hierarchy
    of abstraction, 53
    of goals, 90, 106
    of readiness, 60
    of transition probabilities, 69
Human beings as information sources, 153
Hyperspace, multidimensional, 44
Hypothesis-generation, 53, 70

Ideal language, 93
Imagining, 75
Imperative meaning, 101
Indeterminacy, logical, 132, 147
Indicative meaning of a question, 35, 100
Inductive probability, 81
Information, 10, 14, 19, 56, 70, 76, *80*, 96, 108, 132, *158*
    amount of, 10, 42, 57, 158
    as answer to question, 12
    Fisher's measure of, 4, *169*
    generation of, 137
    humans as sources of, 153
    irrelevant, 74
    operational definition of, 60, 157
    quantization of, 2, 3, 164
    semantic, 19, *79ff*., 89, 95, 107
    source of, 135, 146ff., 153
    space, 44, 92, 169
    and time, 16

units of, 4, 160ff.
vector, 45, 71, 92, 169
Information-content, 56, 157
    descriptive or scientific, 12, 15, 45, 59, 82, *159*
    metrical, 4, 14, 44, 48, 159, *166*
    selective, 10–14, 71, 75, 147, 159, *172*
    semantic, 59, 83
    structural, 14, 159, *165*, *178ff*.
Informational efficiency, 3, 15
Internal organisers, 113
Internal representation, 50, *68*, 112, 125, 142
Interrogative utterances, 31, 97, 107
Intonation, function of, 32, 98
Instructions, 130

Kantian categories, 69

Learning, 70
Linguistic understanding, 121
Logical atomism, 3, 27
Logical dimensionality (of representation), 4, 5, 165, *178ff*.
Logical indeterminacy, 132, 147
Logon, 4, 165
Logon-capacity, 166, 179, 189
Logon-content, 5, 102, 165, *178ff*.

'Magic number 7', 103
Matching response, adaptive, 51, *61–69*, 73, 112, 142
'Mathematical Theory of Communication' (C. E. Shannon), 5, 79, *passim*
Matrix of conditional or transition-probabilities (C.P.M. or T.P.M.), 62, 83, 95, 106
Meaning
    and information, 5, 20, 24, 46, 53, 71, *79*, 83, 91, 96, *108*
    conventional, 25, 84, 90
    definition of, 24, 71, *84*, 128
    effective, received or understood, 25, 72, *84*
    imperative, *101*
    of indicative sentences, 22, 96

intended, 25, 72
interrogative, 35, 100
shades of, 49
spectrum of, 48
symbolic representation of, 72
Meaningfulness, criterion of, 19, 21, 36, *89*
Meaninglessness, 21, 36, *85*, 111, 128
Mechanical translation, 90
Memory, 64–66
Messages as 'keys', 25, 27, 109–111
Metrical information-content, 4, 14, 44, 48, 159, *166*
Metron, metrical unit of information, 5, 166
Microscope, resolving power of, 185
Miller, G. A., 103
Mismatch (in feed-back system), 69
Misunderstanding, 129

Natural selection (of organizing subroutines), 141
Nervous system, 63–66
Noise, 134, 186
in automata, 136
semantic, 74
Numerical energy, 167

Occupance-relations, 2
Observer-language, 58, 61
Operational approach (to information theory), 157
Operationalists, 27ff.
Optical illusions, 69
Optical resolving power, 178, 185
Order-number (of hierarchic level), 102
Organiser, internal, 113
Organising or orienting function, 36, 96ff., 108, 111
Originality, 137

Partial participation (of elements in concept), 47
Pattern of demand, 112
Perception, 61, 68, 96
ambiguities of, 69

Physiological processes, random, 143
Popper, K. S., 153
Potentiation, physiological, 65
Probabilistic artifacts, 54, 140
Probabilities, conditional, 34, 62, 73
Probability-distribution, conditional, 73
Promises, 131

Quantization of information, 2, 3, 164
Quantum of action, 1
Questions, 31, 73, 130

Randomness, 133
Random physiological processes, 143
Reasoning mechanisms, 46, 49
Redundancy, 173
Relative entropy, 173
Relevance (of information), 49, 56, 59, 73, *170*
Religious commitment, 114
Repertoire, 95
Replication (as a form of representation), 50
Representation of meaning, symbolic, 72
Representations, 3, 42, 49, *68*, 80, 89, 112, 158, *161*
Requests, 100, 130
Resolving power
of measurements, 1, 166
optical, 178, 185
Response, matching, 61, 67
Response-space, 73
Russell, B., 27

Scientific experimentation, 11, 14
Scientific information (measures of), 43
Scientific representation, 3, 164ff.
Second law of thermodynamics, 16
Selective function (of message, question), 24, 35, 108
Selective information-content, 10–14, 71, 75, 147, 159, *172*
Self-organisation, 140

196 *INDEX*

Semantic information, information-content, 19, 59, *79ff.*, 95, 107
Semantic noise, 74
Semantic units (and criteria of truthfulness), 28
Shannon, C. E., 5, 19, 43, 59, 79, 94, 171, 184
Social groups, units, 106, 115–118
Spectrum of meaning, 48
Speed of transmission (as adaptive parameter), 66
States of (conditional) readiness, 19, 34, 60, 75, 142
ensemble of, 75
Statistical approximation to English, 139
Stimulus equivalence, 121
Structural information content, 14, 159, *165, 178ff.*
Symbolic representation of meaning, 72
Symbols, basic, internal, 49–54, 113, 141
Synonymy, 86

Temporal relationships in neural networks, 66
Theory of information, glossary of terms used in, 161–177
Thermodynamics and information theory, 16, 174
Thesauri, 103
Threshold configurations (as internal representations), 141
Threshold-control, 65
Time and information, 16

Toraldo di Francia, G., 185, 188–189
'Tractatus Logico-Philosophicus', 2, 27
Transition-probability matrix, 52, 62
Translation, mechanical, 90
Transmission, speed of (as adaptive parameter), 66
Trial and error (adaptive), 69, 72, 142
Truthfulness, criteria of, 28

Uncertainty
absolute, 148, 150, 154
and information content, 147
principles, 1, 146
Understanding, non-linguistic versus linguistic, 121
Unexpectedness as measure of information, 57, 94, 133, 160
Units of information, 4, 160ff.
Universal language, 77
Universals, 53
Unpredictability, 146

Valuative feed-back, 67, 140
Values in relation to communication barriers, 114
Variational approach, 99, 124
Vector representation of information, 44, 71, 92, 169
Vectors, basic, 48, 72
Visual perception, ambiguities of, 69

Warning (as communication), 130
Weight of evidence, 4, 5, 49, 166
Wiener, N., 9, 171
Wittgenstein, L., 2, 27, 30, 164